Dr Johnson & Mrs. Thrale's
Tour in North Wales
1774

To
My Wife

Dr Johnson
&
Mrs Thrale's Tour in North Wales 1774

With an Introduction and Notes

by

Adrian Bristow

Wrexham, Clwyd

Dr Johnson & Mrs Thrale's
Tour in North Wales, 1774
First published in Wales by
BRIDGE BOOKS
61 Park Avenue
Wrexham, Clwyd
LL12 7AW

© 1995 Adrian Bristow

All Rights Reserved.
No part of this publication may be reproduced,
stored in a retrieval system, or transmitted
in any form or by any means, electronic,
mechanical, photocopying, recording or
otherwise, without the prior permission
of the Copyright holder.

ISBN 1-872424-49-X

A CIP catalogue entry for this book
is available from the British Library

Printed and bound by
MFP, Stretford, Manchester

Contents

List of Maps & Illustrations	6
Preface	7
Introduction	11
Preamble	11
The Party	13
The Bachygraig Inheritance	18
The Diaries	19
The Diaries Compared	21
Aftermath	25
A Journey into North Wales in the Year 1774 by Samuel Johnson	29
Notes on Dr. Johnson's Diary	57
Journal of a Tour in Wales with Dr. Johnson by Mrs. Thrale	87
Notes on Mrs. Thrale's Journal	127
Select Bibliography	143
Index	144

LIST OF MAPS AND ILLUSTRATIONS

Route from London to Mold	9
The Tour of North Wales	10
Mr. Henry Thrale	14
Mrs. Thrale	16
Mrs. Thrale's Journal	20
Samuel Johnson, L.L.D.	30
Lleweni Hall in 1789	37
St. Winifride's Well, Holywell in 1830	40
The Grammar School, Beaumaris	46
Caernarfon Castle	48
Dolbadarn Castle	50
The Cathedral Church of St. Deiniol, Bangor	51
The Parish Church of St. Giles, Wrexham	53
The Terrace at Llannerch	69
The Parish Church of St. Beuno, Clynnog Fawr	77
The Stable Block, Lleweni Hall	101
Bachygraig in 1776	102
16th c. Barn at Bachygraig	102
Gwaynynog: the South Front	106
Dr. Johnson's Urn, Gwaynynog	107
Maesmynnan	108
Part of Fort Williamsburg, Glynllifon	114
Bodfel Hall, Llannor	115
The Parish Church, Llannor	116
Mr. John Myddleton of Gwaynynog	119
The Memorial Plaque, Tremeirchion Church	133

Preface

Writing this book has involved much travelling in agreeable areas and visits to many places I had never seen before. In preparing the notes, I have followed as diligently as possible in the tracks of the touring party. I have visited every house, church, ruin, farm, park, monument, lake, cathedral, castle, chapel and location mentioned by Johnson and Mrs. Thrale. In those cases where I have not actually been inside a building, I have carefully observed it from the outside. Like many earnest seekers, I have occasionally been frustrated by finding country churches locked against theft and vandalism with, occasionally, no indication of where the key might be found.

Where appropriate, I have compared what Johnson and Mrs. Thrale saw with what the traveller sees today. If some of the notes are rather extensive, I hope I have been able to provide details of persons, buildings and places mentioned in the diaries that were previously not available.

I suppose one always hopes that, in following in the footsteps of such an illustrious and indomitable pair, one may find some previously undiscovered letter, picture or relic of their tour. Sadly, I failed to come across anything of the kind, apart from one dubious Johnsonian article – see Johnson Note 107. What I did find rather surprising was that most of the country houses visited by the party were still largely untouched by the passage of over two centuries. Some were even owned by the same family, while others had become schools or colleges, flats or various types of institution.

Johnson and Mrs. Thrale travelled through a landscape in North Wales virtually innocent of industrial development. Ironically, the only industrial area existing at that time which they visited, the Holywell valley on Deeside, is now a quiet, green backwater. Although tourism and residential development, plus the impact of extractive industries, have severely damaged the North Wales coast, fortunately the hinterland remains unspoilt and mainly unchanged.

For those readers interested in the history of garden design and the development in the eighteenth century of 'landscape painting', the party visited several of the most influential gardens and estates of the period, including Baron Hill, Hagley, The Leasowes and Blenheim.

I hope that some of those who read this book may be encouraged to follow the jolting Johnsonian coach up through the Midlands, across the Cheshire plain and over the hills into the quiet lanes of the Vale of Clwyd. Beyond lie the great Edwardian castles, the Menai Strait, Snowdonia, Anglesey and the pleasures of the Lleyn peninsula. One could hardly wish for two more spirited companions on such a journey.

Of the many people who helped me in the preparation of this book, I should like particularly to acknowledge the kindness and assistance of the following:-

Mr. & Mrs. Arthur Pennant of Nantlys, Tremeirchion.
Mr. & Mrs. T. Smith of Gwaynynog.
Mrs. S. Gordon of Cefn-Mine, Pwllheli.
Miss C. M. Ritchie, Librarian, University College, Oxford.
Miss Kate Arnold-Foster, Museum Curator,
Royal Pharmaceutical Society of Great Britain.
Miss R. Ensing.
Mr. A. Champion.

Adrian Bristow
Chester, 1995

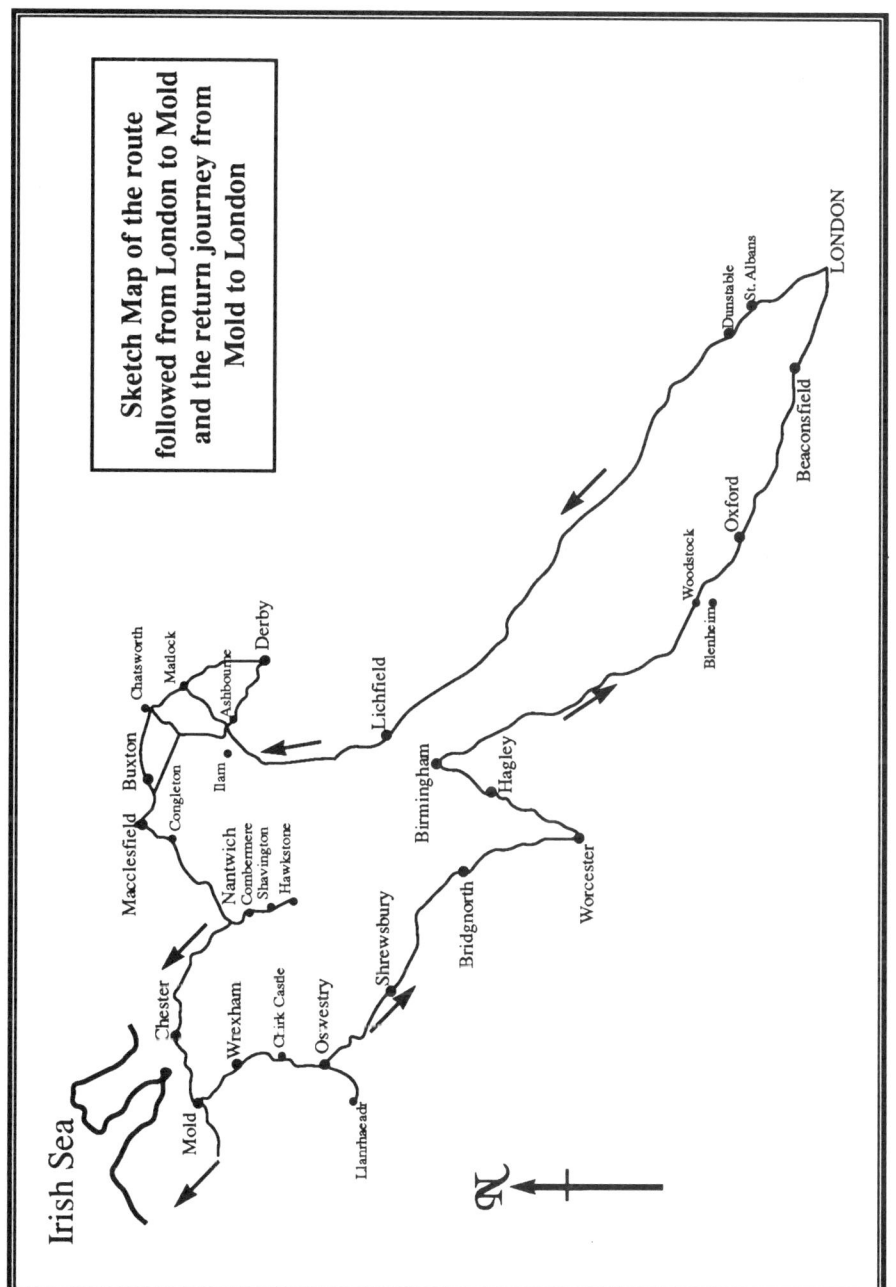

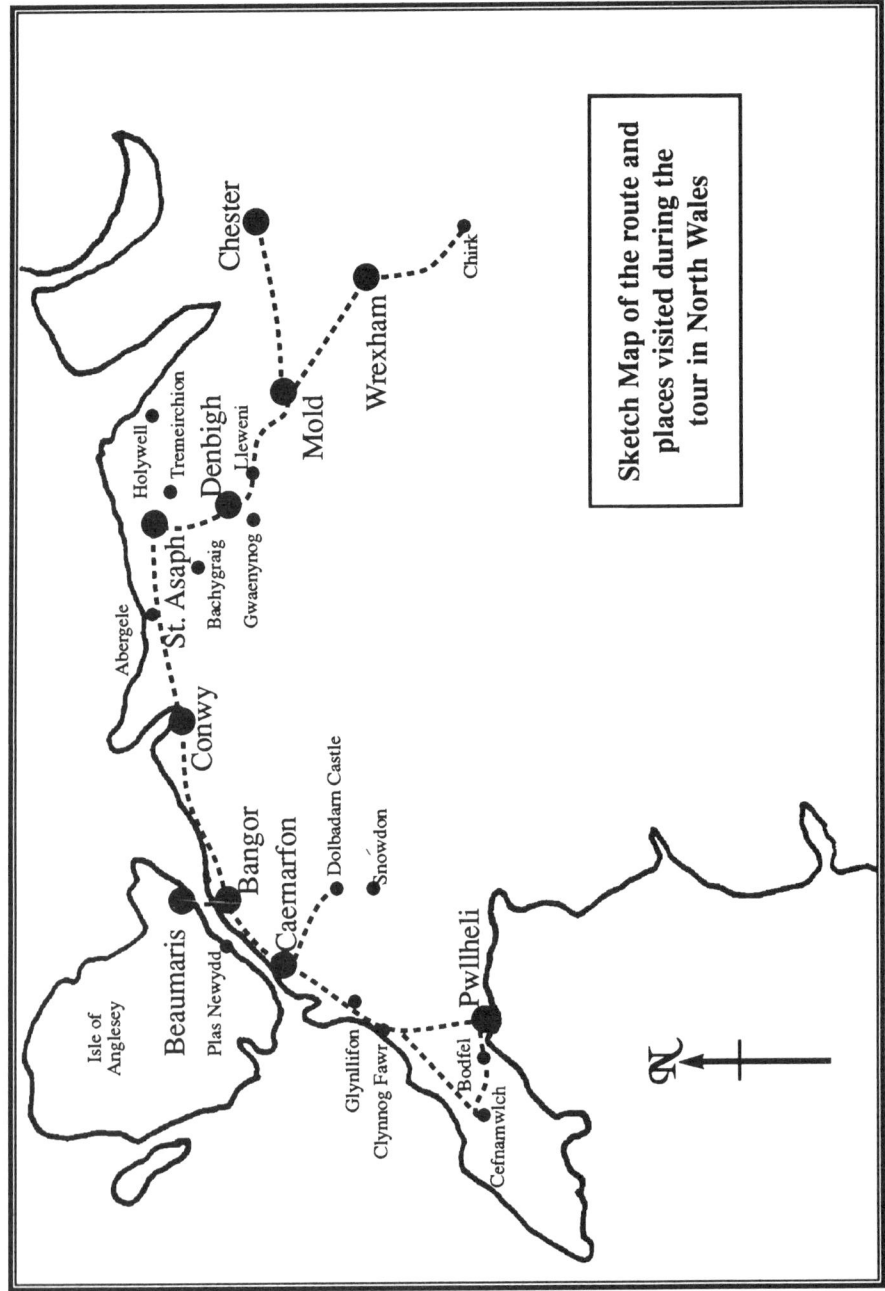

Sketch Map of the route and places visited during the tour in North Wales

Introduction

Preamble

All his life Johnson had wanted to travel, especially to visit the cradles of European civilization. As he observed to Boswell: "The grand object of travelling is to see the shores of the Mediterranean. On those shores were the four great empires of the world; the Assyrian, the Persian, the Grecian and the Roman. – All our religion, almost all our law, almost all our arts, almost all that sets us above savages, has come to us from the shores of the Mediterranean." He often talked about visiting different countries and the various benefits to be derived thereby, yet he was forced to remain an armchair traveller. For twenty-five years of his working life, as he toiled away in Grub Street, he had neither the time nor the money for travel. During this period he barely stirred outside the capital except for infrequent visits to his wife and friends in Oxford, Lichfield and Derby. But in 1762 George III granted him a pension of three hundred pounds a year for his services to letters. Johnson was at last freed from hardship and was able to live more comfortably and to contemplate the possibility of going abroad.

In 1765 he was introduced to Mr. and Mrs. Thrale, and the acquaintnace rapidly ripened into an intimate friendship. Discussions with the lively Mrs. Thrale gave fresh impetus to his desire to see new places and unfamiliar scenes since neither of them had ever set foot outside England. Yet, although he was financially secure, it was not until 1773 that he finally agreed to Boswell's repeated suggestion that the two men should visit the Scottish Highlands and the Western Isles. Johnson enjoyed the tour tremendously, despite the rigours and dangers of the journey, and it sharpened his appetite for further adventures. As he remarked later in a letter to an old friend, John Taylor, on 16 November, 1775, "Is not mine a kind of life turned upside down? Fixed to a spot when I was young, and roving the world when others are contriving to sit still, I am wholly unsettled. I am a kind of ship with a wide sail, and without an anchor."

The following year he was particularly eager to visit Italy. Mrs. Thrale was equally enthusiastic and they discussed various itineraries until Henry Thrale put an end to their project by declaring that by far the most important journey to be undertaken was to North Wales. This would enable Mrs. Thrale to take possession of her family estate at Bachygraig, near Denbigh, which she had recently inherited following the death of her uncle, Sir Thomas Salusbury. With business and pleasure being thus agreeably united, he had no objection to their visit being developed into a sightseeing tour. As usual, Thrale's view prevailed; not unreasonably perhaps, since he would be paying the expenses of the tour.

Mrs. Thrale fell in with his idea because she needed to take stock of her new property and to settle several problems connected with the management of it. She also looked forward to revisiting the area in which she had spent part of her childhood for another reason. She was eager to unfold to Johnson the beauties of North Wales and she felt confident these would rival the splendours of the Western Highlands which he had seen the previous summer. She very much wanted to see what effect these new prospects would have upon him and how he would respond.

Above all, she badly needed a change and to get away from London. The previous year had been a sad and depressing one. Her mother, whom she dearly loved, died in June after a long and painful struggle with cancer and in November her four year old daughter, Lucy, who had been unwell for some time, suddenly sickened and died of mastoiditis. In her Family Book, which began as a journal dealing with her children's development, she wrote: "So Farewell to all I formerly loved – to my Mother, my House in Hertfordshire, my lovely Lucy – and to this accursed Year 1773." This tour, when she would have the redoubtable Johnson all to herself for several weeks, was intended, apart from the business element, to be both a holiday of the spirit and a nostalgic return to the places she had known and loved as a girl.

Johnson, accepting Thrale's decision as he usually did, was content to postpone the cherished visit to Italy, even if he did not entirely share Mrs. Thrale's enthusiasm for going to North Wales.

Their plans gradually took shape. On the way north to Chester the party would first visit Johnson's home town of Lichfield, where he would introduce the Thrales to his relatives and friends and arrange a programme of visits. Then they would spend a few days at Ashbourne in Derbyshire with John Taylor, one of his oldest friends, before going on to Combermere Abbey near Nantwich to stay with Sir Lynch Salusbury Cotton, Mrs. Thrale's uncle. From there they would proceed to Lleweni Hall near Denbigh to spend three weeks with Robert Cotton, Sir Lynch's son and Mrs. Thrale's cousin. Here Mrs. Thrale, in her turn, would introduce Johnson to her friends and to places of interest, while she and her husband attempted to resolve problems arising from her inheritance of Bachygraig. Later the party would drive along the difficult North Wales coast road and through Caernarfonshire to Mrs. Thrale's birthplace at Bodfel Hall outside Pwllheli. They would return by the same coastal route and make their way back to London via Shrewsbury, Birmingham and Oxford.

Johnson expected to be away from London for about five weeks but in the end the tour was to take a little over two months.

The Party

The party was to consist of Johnson, Mr. & Mrs. Thrale and their eldest daughter, Queeney. At this time Henry Thrale was fifty years old, his wife, thirty three, Queeney ten, and Johnson sixty four.

Henry Thrale, the son of a wealthy brewer, had been educated at Eton and Oxford and was regarded, despite one or two financial near-disasters, as a successful business man. At this time he was the Member of Parliament for Southwark where he also had a house in Deadman's Place, near the family brewery. He was a handsome man, with conventional views and attitudes which he showed little inclination to alter. He enjoyed the pleasures of the table and the bedroom and believed that woman was created for his delight in both. He had certain admirable traits but they were not necessarily endearing ones; certainly he was cordially disliked by his father-in-law who had once sworn he would not have his daughter exchanged for a barrel of porter. He had also stormed at his daughter, "If you marry that Scoundrel he will catch the pox and for your Amusement set you to make his Pultices." Thrale did both in due course.

He was considered cold and undemonstrative by many, a characteristic underlined by a firm and decided manner. He was one of the very few unafraid to silence Johnson when he began to be tiresome, yet he and Johnson seemed to get on together well enough. Johnson admired him as a well-educated and successful man of business in public life, while in private life: "I know of no man who is more master of his wife and family than Thrale. If he but holds up a finger he is obeyed". Thrale liked good talk though he contributed little himself; Johnson felt sure he could have done so to some effect.

Mrs. Thrale, writing two years after the tour in North Wales, has left us a dispassionate appraisal of her husband:

"Mr. Thrale's person is manly, his countenance agreeable, his eyes steady and of the deepest blue; his look neither soft nor severe, neither sprightly nor gloomy, but thoughtful and intelligent; his address is neither caressive nor repulsive, but unaffectedly civil and decorous; and his manner more completely free from every kind of trick or particularity than I ever saw any person's ...

"Mr. Thrale's sobriety, and the decency of his conversation, being wholly free from all oaths, ribaldry and profaneness, make him a man exceedingly comfortable to live with; while the easiness of his temper and slowness to take offence add greatly to his value as a domestic man. Yet I think his servants do not love him, and I am not sure that his children have much affection for him; low people almost all indeed agree to abhor him, as he has none of that officious

Mr. Henry Thrale.

and cordial manner which is universally required by them, nor any skill to dissemble his dislike of their coarseness. With regard to his wife, though little tender of her person, he is very partial to her understanding; but he is obliging to nobody, and confers a favour less pleasingly than many a man refuses to confer one. This appears to me to be as just a character as can be given of the man with whom I have now lived thirteen years; and though he is extremely reserved and uncommunicative, yet one must know something of him after so long an acquaintance. Johnson has a very great degree of kindness and esteem for him, and says if he would talk more, his manner would be very completely that of a perfect gentleman."

Hester Thrale made a startling contrast to her husband. Barely five feet tall and slightly built (she was described not too kindly by Boswell as being "short, plump, and brisk"), she was highly intelligent, articulate and vivacious. She was the only child of John Salusbury of Bachygraig, a handsome, irresponsible and irascible fellow. Unable to live on his debt-ridden estate, her parents spent their early married life at Bodfel Hall, haunted by a lack of money stemming from

John's inability to establish himself in a career or to profit from the opportunities presented to him.

Mrs. Thrale, taught by a sympathetic and civilised mother, was widely read and her precocious literary tastes had been encouraged by her wealthy relatives. While her father was attempting, with little success, to repair his fortunes in the New World, she and her mother lived for much of their time, once they had escaped from the isolation and penury of Bodfel Hall, on the estates of their relatives at Lleweni Hall, Combermere Abbey, and Offley Place. Mrs. Thrale was intensely interested in, and inordinately proud of, her ancestors, and it was one of the few topics on which her wide acquaintance found her tedious. Her marriage to Henry Thrale (which she had embraced with little enthusiasm) was, despite his emotional limitations, not an unhappy one, even though he did keep her in a perpetual state of pregnancy for years.

She first met Johnson in 1765. Each developed an understandable fascination for the other and within a short time Johnson was a part-time resident at the Thrales' country house at Streatham. Here she encouraged him to bring his London friends, drawn from the beau monde of politics, art, and the theatre, and she delighted in the brilliance of the Johnson circle.

The Thrale's eldest daughter, Hester Maria, had been called "Queeney" as a small child by Johnson (after Queen Esther) and the nickname stuck, though her mother occasionally called her Niggy, Nig or Hetty. Johnson, who loved small children, was very fond of her, teasing her and calling her "Puss", but she was not an easy child to love at times. Besides being precocious and obstinate, she had inherited something of her father's temperament and could be cold and unresponsive in company. Sadly, she neither grew out of this nor mellowed with age, and there are references to her glacial charm in later life. She married George Elphinstone, Lord Keith, in 1808 and, enjoying her mother's constitution, lived until she was ninety-two.

On the eve of their departure, having made arrangements for the care of her family, Mrs. Thrale wrote:

"Tomorrow we set forward on our Journey to Wales; Yesterday, – no! this very Morning I set Sophy safe at Kensington with her Sister, who is so altered for the better it quite charms me; I never saw any thing like the Improvement only from March–July – 'tis incredible. Yet I am very lowspirited at leaving them, - the two Boys too – what will become of them? Ralph is just eight Months old, a fine Boy to look at, but strangely backward somehow in his Understanding – however if he lives & thrives - that will come; Old Nurse doats upon him & will I am sure be careful; my sweet Harry! I have ordered him to board at Thomas's School during our Absence, and come home only to bed; – for I thought he might take Liberties of chusing his own Dinners if he tabled here, and not only eat too much

16   Dr Johnson & Mrs. Thrale's Tour in North Wales 1774

Mrs. Thrale.

perhaps & of improper Things – but turn his Mind too much towards his Belly the only Fault I think he naturally has.

I can do no better for them all, yet somehow I am not satisfied with myself: had my Mother been living perhaps I had done better; perhaps I have lost my Virtue with my Parent: She would not have approved my leaving them & then I should not have gone. I shall now perhaps neglect them more & more – Oh God forbid! and grant us if it be thy blessed will, a happy meeting at my return from Wales. I cannot write for crying tonight, I am so very low spirited: I shall perhaps be better in the Morning. Adieu to my Dear Children then!* – Adieu indeed, for to God's care do I commit them – late at night."

The next day, before the coach carried them northwards, Johnson wrote to his friend Bennet Langton: "I have just begun to print my Journey to the Hebrides,+ and am leaving the press to take another journey into Wales whither Mr. Thrale is going, to take possession of, at least, five hundred a year, fallen to his lady. All at Streatham, that are alive, are well. I have never recovered from the last dreadful illness but flatter myself that I have grown gradually better; much, however, yet remains to mend."

The journey into the extremities of North Wales was, like the previous year's excursion to Scotland, not one to be undertaken lightly. The roads in North Wales were certainly not as appalling as those in the highlands of Scotland where, once one left the military roads driven in by General Wade, one was faced with what were only tracks across a vast expanse of hills and moor and bog. It is difficult to appreciate the condition of our roads at this period. Indeed, the term 'road' is inappropriate except for stretches of those arteries radiating from London. Once away from these highways the traveller was faced with narrow lanes that were either a frequently impassable morass in winter or a deeply-rutted, boulder-strewn hazard in summer. Bridges were few and rivers and estuaries had to be crossed in open boats often under dangerous conditions. There were very few carriages to be seen in North Wales and these, like the Thrales's splendid equipage, had to be carried across rivers in large ferry-boats or had to wait for low tide to pass round disobliging headlands. For travellers who were ill or feeling unwell, like Johnson and Mrs. Thrale at times, coach travel was a slow, exhausting and highly disagreeable experience. That this is not remarked upon unduly by our two diarists suggests that they had become too inured to it over the years to complain.

* Sophia b. 23 July 1771, Susanna Arabella b. 23 May 1770; Ralph b. 8 Nov. 1775, who was to die in December; Henry (Harry) Salusbury b. 15Feb. 1767, her elder son, and Thrale's heir, who was to die two years later.

+ This was his account of his Scottish tour made with Boswell the previous year and published as *A Journey to the Western Islands of Scotland* in 1775.

Despite Johnson's lingering doubts about his health and any misgivings Mrs. Thrale might have had about the organisation of the venture, there were no serious problems to cloud the summer skies. The party left the Thrales's house in Streatham in good spirits on a bright morning on Tuesday, 5th July, 1774, in the family's comfortable coach, on a bright bright morning. This harmony lasted throughout a long and tiring day, but no longer. During the next two days Mrs. Thrale was quite put out by Johnson's behaviour – and Queeney had already caught the first of several colds.

Before we follow the party's progress towards North Wales it might be helpful to set out as simply as possible the background of Mrs. Thrale's inheritance of Bachygraig, since it is referred to on numerous occasions in her diary.

The Bachygraig Inheritance

Mrs. Thrale's family, the Salusburys, had owned the Bachygraig estate for generations and it eventually passed into the hands of Hester's father, John Salusbury (1707-62). At the time of his marriage to his cousin, Hester Maria Cotton, in 1738, the estate, in the absence of any direct male heirs of John, was entailed on his brother, Thomas, later to become Sir Thomas Salusbury. Shortly afterwards John was forced to leave Bachygraig because his extravagance and fecklessness had virtually ruined the estate. He and his wife went to live at Bodfel Hall, near Pwllheli, where their only child, Hester Lynch Salusbury, was born on 16 January, 1741. John had left the affairs of the estate in the hands of his agent, Edward Bridge. For many years Bridge attempted to appease or pay off creditors while trying to manage a property chronically short of funds. He also took care to ensure a comfortable living for himself.

In 1755, Thomas, who had prospered as a result of a fortunate marriage, paid off the £6,000 mortgage on the estate, a not entirely altruistic act on his part since he stood to inherit it, as there was little likelihood of his brother John producing an heir. John, who had continued to fail dismally in life, died suddenly in 1762, Sir Thomas duly came into possession of Bachygraig, cleared the debts once again and made modest provision for Mrs. Salusbury and Hester. Since by this time Sir Thomas was a widower and had no male heir, Hester was next-in-line to inherit Bachygraig. More important, she was confidently regarded as the heir to Sir Thomas's estate at Offley as well.

However, to general surprise, though surprises of this kind are frequently sprung by widowers, Sir Thomas suddenly married a widow (a Mrs. King) and Hester's expectations were dashed. So when Sir Thomas died shortly afterwards in 1773 his main property at Offley in Hertfordshire and his entire personal estate went to the new Lady Salusbury. Since he still had no heir, Hester at least

Introduction 19

inherited Bachygraig, although, under the law at that time, the estate became the property of her husband.

The Diaries

Johnson's Diary was never intended for publication. It eventually found its way into the possession of the Rev. Henry White. He wrote to Dr. Robert Myddleton of Gwaynynog on 7 Jan. 1813, asking him to draw its existence to the notice of Mrs. Piozzi* then living nearby at Brynbella. "I have not the least doubt of my making what is called a good thing of its publication – but God forbid that I should .... for the *lucre* of gain commit the High Character of Johnson's pen by the publication of what He might have intended to keep from the Public Eye." Myddleton got in touch with Mrs. Piozzi, who in due course met the two men, examined the manuscript and commented in a letter to Queeney, now Lady Keith, on 15 May, 1813: "Did I mention to dear Lady Keith a literary curiosity that was shown me in Town? The Journal Doctor Johnson kept of our Tour in Wales? If the proprietor resolves to print it, he must exchange Peace for Pelf, and so I had the honour to tell him." According to Mrs. Piozzi, White "repeatedly observed he would print it, only it was not sufficiently bulky for publication." However, he eventually abandoned the idea and the Diary passed into the hands of Richard Duppa who resolved to publish it.

In his Dedication to Edward Swinbourne in the Preface, Duppa wrote: "This fragment, as a literary curiosity, I hope will not disappoint you; for although it may not contain any striking and important facts, or luminous passages of fine writing, it cannot be uninteresting to know how the mind of such a man as Johnson received new impressions, or contemplated for the first time, scenes and occupations unknown to him before".

Duppa had the benefit of corresponding with a still active and vivacious Mrs. Piozzi to clarify certain entries and discrepancies in the text. His edition of Johnson's Diary appeared in 1816 but it still contained many inaccuracies. Shortly after publication Mrs. Piozzi wrote: "Johnson's Diary is selling rapidly, though the contents are *bien maigre*, I must confess. Mr. Duppa has sent me the book, and I perceive has politely suppressed some sarcastic expressions about my family, the Cottons, whom we visited at Combermere and at Lleweney."

In 1831 more notes were added by John Wilson Croker, who collated his first edition with the original MS and included it in subsequent editions of his *Life of Johnson*. In preparing Johnson's Diary I have followed the masterly Hill-Powell edition of the text contained in Volume V of *Boswell's Life of Johnson* (Oxford,

---

* Mrs. Thrale remarried after Thrale's death and became Mrs. Piozzi. See N.B. on page 127.

On Tuesday 5. July 1774 I began my Journey through Wales, We set out from Streatham in our Coach & four post Horses accompanied by Mr. Johnson and our eldest Daughter. Baretti went with us as far as London where we left him, & hiring fresh Horses. they carried us to the Mitre at Barnet, a House kept by Lady Lade's Maid with whom I left a Letter for her quondam Mistress. At St Albans we were hospitably received by Ralph Smith & his Wife relations to Mr Thrale who gave us a good cold Dinner, and from whom we had much Trouble to get away to a Sister of theirs who has another House in the Town and detained us to drink Tea with her & her Son. There I was first made to Observe the apparent degeneration of the Wild Pheasants Plumage when rendered Domestic. In the Afternoon we drove on to Dunstable, where we spent the Night, after a Day in which nothing had been learned, said done or known, but the passing through a Space of 40 Miles from home with Emotions perpetually changing & perpetually strong. every Sign, every Bush, every Stone almost reminding us of Time

The first page from Mrs. Thrale's Journal of her Welsh Tour.

1964). Like all writers about Johnson, I hasten to acknowledge my debt here.

R. W. Chapman, beguiled into adopting an almost Johnsonian tone, comments in the introduction to his edition of *The Letters of Samuel Johnson*, "that the great biographer did not in his own practice achieve a consistent orthography, and was conspicuously careless about proper names. Some of his idiosyncracies, however, have a certain consistency, notably his avoidance of double final consonants e.g. Boswel." He also admits that Johnson's handwriting is often puzzling, even to experts.

I have kept Johnson's spelling and erratic punctuation but I have given the modern spelling of Welsh place-names and certain proper names at their first appearance. A few minor slips and omissions are indicated by square brackets. In the original Diary (the MS is in the British Museum) the pages are divided into two columns; Johnson writes his entries in both columns, but occasionally he uses the right hand column for odd notes and comments. These I have integrated with the text where desirable.

Nothing was known of Mrs. Thrale's Journal until 1908 when the original MS appeared as Lot 778, 'Welch Journal 1774', at the sale of Mrs. Piozzi's MSS at Sotheby's on 4 June. It was bought by Quaritch and then passed into the hands of A. M. Broadley. The 'Journal', edited by Broadley, was published by The Bodley Head in the following year in a book called *Dr. Johnson and Mrs. Thrale*, which also contained Johnson's Diary and much other material.Her Journal has not been published since then. Mrs. Thrale's handwriting is wonderfully neat and clear and I have followed Bradley's transcription, with certain exceptions which I have noted in the text.

Throughout her 'Journal' Mrs. Thrale refers to Johnson as "Mr. Johnson"; interestingly, Johnson declined to assume the title of 'Doctor' and continued to call himself 'Mr. Johnson'. Boswell thought it might have been because he sometimes preferred to be taken not as a literary figure but as *"un gentilhomme comme un autre"*. A few minutes spent in the Great Cham's company would have soon exploded that idea.

The Diaries Compared

Mrs. Thrale's 'Journal' was the first of her travel journals and was not written for publication. Vastly more entertaining than Johnson's own Diary, it reflects her personality – lively, shrewd, emotional, and rarely dull. She is no Boswell, however. She was concerned with recording her own impressions not those of Johnson, though she does comment on his attitude and activities. Her Journal is a chronicle of events, places and people, enlivened by waspish observations on most of the men and women she encountered. Her sharp tongue is matched by a caustic pen and she spares neither acquaintances nor relatives. For example, she deplores Henry Thrale's selfishness and insensitivity and she is irritated on occasions by Johnson's tiresome behaviour. One suspects he was beginning to weary her towards the end of their rather lengthy tour. She casts a trained eye upon a badly-managed household and no disappointing table escapes her. Nearly two years later in March, 1776, Boswell visited Lichfield, Ashbourne, Birmingham, and Oxford with Johnson and met a number of the people mentioned by Mrs. Thrale. Although Boswell's comments in his *Life of Samuel Johnson* fall outside the scope of this book, they underline the acuteness of Mrs. Thrale's eye, ear, and pen.

Her 'Journal' includes some sentimental and melancholy passages induced by visits to her birthplace and to places which held happy associations for her, but these are not out of place in a private diary. There are also entries revealing her anxiety about her family. Her concern for Queeney and her other children left behind at Streatham goes some way to soften her uncertain reputation as an affectionate mother.

Boswell was pretty certain that Johnson did not keep a diary on his tour of North Wales, but he was wrong. He should have known better, because not only was Johnson an inveterate note-taker and recorder himself but he was much given to advising his friends to do the same.

Yet what are we to make of Johnson's published journal? It is interesting, first, to consider it in relation to the other two diaries he kept of his travels, in Scotland (1773) and in France (1775). He used the diary he kept during his expedition with Boswell to the Highlands as the basis for his successful travel book, *Journey to the Western Isles*. Unfortunately, this diary is lost so we do not know what it looked like, but it is possible that it resembled the one he kept in France two years later. Although the first part of that diary, too, is lost, Boswell printed the remains of it in his *Life of Samuel Johnson*.

What survives of the French diary is a brief but fascinating record of visits made, persons met, and sights seen for a period of twenty-six days, much of it in the form of staccato, Jingle-type jottings. Perhaps his Scottish diary was cast in this form, for there is no reason why his French notes could not have been expanded, elaborated upon, and fashioned into an attractive travel book had he so wished. Boswell certainly thought that Johnson's two months' stay in France might produce another slim volume. "Shall we have 'A Journey to Paris' from you in the winter?", he wrote to him on 24th October 1775. It was not to be; the tantalising glimpses we have of Johnson and the Thrales at the court of Louis XVI and Marie-Antoinette at Fontainebleau only suggest what might have been.

Johnson's *A Journey into North Wales*, however, is not like this. It is a curiously uneven piece of work, both in quality and quantity. It is certainly no aide-memoire, no collection of facts or record of impressions from which he would later be able to construct at leisure a detailed narrative of his travels. He makes, for example, few entries of any substance, except for a description of a visit to Hawkstone Park, until he is well into his stay at Lleweni in North Wales. This is understandable since, on his way there, the days he passed at Lichfield and Ashbourne were spent in meeting old friends and visiting places he had known for years. Again, as one might expect, the diary falls away lamentably at the end of August after his stay at Gwaynynog when he returns to the familiar towns of Shrewsbury, Birmingham and Oxford.

Many of the entries relating to North Wales are but brief records of activity or humdrum accounts of the party's excursions. Occasionally we find quite lengthy passages, such as his description of Holywell or the journey to Bangor via Penmaenmawr, which could quite easily have been included in a book without much alteration. Overall, there is not the interest in the minutiae of daily life or in things seen that he displayed in his earlier travel book. Nor is it easy to pick out comments or details that would have generated those splendid and reverberating observations on men, manners and morals that we find in his *Journey to the Western Isles*.

In a letter to Boswell about their Scottish tour Johnson declared, "our business was with life and manners", but there is too little of this in his North Wales diary. Thomas Roscoe certainly thought so. Roscoe was a writer and translator whose *Wanderings in North Wales* (1836) covered much of the area travelled by Johnson. He commented: "The rough diary kept by the Doctor is very dull and heavy, with but few gleams of vivacity, and less sterling merit as a record of the intellectual leviathan of his Age. It fills up a chasm, indeed, of his life; but it is chiefly with rubbish, scarcely worth the observation of his biographers." As we have seen, Mrs. Piozzi shared this view though she expressed it more tactfully.

One wonders whether, in fact, Johnson intended to produce a book based upon his experiences. This may well have been in his mind at the start but it seems that any enthusiasm for the project waned as the weeks slipped by. He may have become more than a little bored with a tour that had promised much but had yielded relatively little to his taste. Perhaps he felt that after Scotland everything else was an anti-climax. There, Boswell had promised him that he would experience an entirely different way of life and would "find simplicity and wildness, and all the circumstances of remote time and place". All this was realised. There, to his satisfaction, he had encountered a country "fertile of novelty", with an almost feudal society painfully coming to terms with the changes brought about by the defeat of the '45 rebellion and the repression which followed it. Travelling had been arduous and occasionally dangerous, and he sometimes had to stay in miserable inns and cottages where the food was as unwholesome as the beds. In North Wales, on the other hand, he travelled in some state with the Thrales, staying mainly in comfortable country-houses belonging to Mrs. Thrale's friends or relatives. Thus he had little contact with ordinary people and rarely entered a humble dwelling.

Wales seemed to offer little of the excitement and opportunity for adventure he had enjoyed in Scotland. There was nothing in this tour to compare with meeting Highland chieftains in their ancient strongholds, riding over Rannoch Moor, or tossing about in a small boat in the stormy waters between Skye and Mull. He had seen more majestic mountains and more spectacular landscapes in Scotland, while he found little of the remoteness and strangeness of the Western Isles in Wales. Wales was too civilised, too like England, to be remarkable, and, much as he enjoyed the lively company of Mrs.Thrale, he missed Boswell. There was no Boswell to prick him on, to play upon his prejudices or to involve him in unusual situations and adventures.

It should be borne in mind that Johnson was now in his mid-sixties. Though his pleasure in travelling remained as keen as ever, certain aspects of his health were worrying him. Besides his major infirmities, he was becoming increasingly deaf and his eyes were troubling him at this time. Ever since infancy Johnson had suffered from myopia, which he felt was the result of scrofula, though it is strange that he appears not to have sought the help of spectacles. He was unwell on several occasions during the tour and this, or simple boredom or a lack of anything significant to record, may account for the days when there are no diary entries. Physically he does not seem quite the man who stood up so stoutly to the rigours of the Highlands and Islands the previous year.

Whatever the cause or causes, at times he simply could not summon up either the energy or the interest to make his usual notes and observations. Once back in the capital he showed little inclination to write a detailed account of his travels.

Boswell might have been expected to ask Johnson if he had kept a diary and, if so, whether he intended to make a book of it. But he did not, nor did he press the matter, merely commenting, "I do not find that he kept any journal or notes of what he saw there." It seems likely that Boswell, who was a little uncomfortable with Mrs. Thrale and already aware of her as a possible rival, was none too keen to encourage the publication of a travel book in which she might cut some kind of figure. There is only a brief reference to the Welsh tour in his *Life of Samuel Johnson* and his attitude towards it, judging by his later comments, was rather dismissive.

It would be wrong to be too severe in our criticism of Johnson's 'Journal'. It was never meant for publication as it stood and Johnson never bothered to develop it further. We are comparing Mrs. Thrale's fluent, personalised account with a rough record, incomplete, uncertain of purpose and unequal in content. However, any record of such a tour left by the great man, no matter how brief or unsatisfactory, must be of some interest and value, particularly if, as in this case, it can be laid beside Mrs. Thrale's Journal, day by day and page by page. As Boswell once declared: "People would like to read what you say of anything". In Duppa's phrase, it remains "a literary curiosity". Even so, I need hardly emphasise the pleasure in comparing in the two narratives the reactions of Johnson and Mrs. Thrale to the people and places they encountered on their tour.

Aftermath

On their return journey to London the party was staying with Edmund Burke at his country house, 'Gregories', in Beaconsfield when news came of the dissolution of Parliament. Mr. Thrale had thus to hurry everyone back to Southwark to start his election campaign; Johnson was to write his election address and Mrs. Thrale prepared to canvass. Back home at Streatham she was delighted to see her children again and badly wanted to spend some time quietly with them, but she found herself whirled off to Southwark. She noted in her Family Book on 30th September:

"I returned safe home from my long Tour; brought Queeney safe back, called on my Girls at Kensington, whom I found quite well; (I had no Time to examine mental Improvements.) and got in good Time to Streatham where Harry met & rejoyced over us very kindly: he is wonderfully grown & seems in perfect health tho' having lost a few Teeth gives him an odd Look, but he appears happy & chearful, and full of Spirits. Little Ralph is more visibly improved than any of 'em, except Susan; who now commences both Wit and Beauty forsooth; She is in no respect the same Child She was two or three Years ago: so that if She did not grow very like Harry, I tell Mrs. Cumyns I should think She had changed her. Every thing however happens to perplex me, & now that I hoped to come home & be quiet examine my Children & see what deficiencies could be supplied, and enjoy a little Quiet after the hurrying Life I have been leading of late – here is the General Election broke out, deuce take it! – and my Attendance is wanted in the Borough."

She also felt compelled to enter a character sketch of Queeney, a compulsion brought on by spending over two months constantly in her company. Making allowances for a certain irritation, it is as chillingly accurate as her description of her husband's personality.

2: Oct

Before I launch into this new Confusion let me mention a Word of my little ones; Queeney kept her Birthday running about Hagley Park. She was pretty well all the

Journey, except a severe Cold & cough whilst we were at Ashburne, & now & then a Slight Touch of the Worms, but nothing really formidable. Upon the whole She has been active, intrepid and observing: & tho' we may have lost some Italian, we have I think gained some Images which will make more than amends. Nothing escapes this Girl's penetration, nothing intimidates her Courage, nothing flutters her Fancy. – Mean Inns, or splendid Apartments – for we have experienced both, find her Mind always prepared to enjoy the one & to defy the other. Mr Johnson tells how She wished to see a Storm when we cross'd over to Anglesey, & how She rode 15 Miles once on a Single hard Trotting in the Night among the Mountains of Snowdon. These are certainly noble Qualities and great performances for a Girl scarce ten Years old, yet is Queeney no very desirable Companion –

Sullen, malicious & perverse; desirous of tormenting me even by hurting herself, & resolute to utter nothing in my hearing, that might give Credit to either of us. She often tells me what She thought on such an Occasion what She could have said &c. when we are alone, but has an affectation of playing the Agnes* when we are in Company together. However when my Back is turned, & She sees no Danger of giving me any Delight, her Tongue is voluble enough I find, & her Manner so particularly pleasing, that a Young Fellow[+] who saw her in Derbyshire half a Dozen times persuaded his foolish Father at his Return to propose him to marry her; protesting he would rather wait seven Years for Miss Thrale, than have any other Girl he ever saw in his Life. – an early Conquest I must confess! so much for Hetty, or Queeney or Niggey as we called Her.

The tour had been deeply disappointing for Mrs. Thrale. She had hoped for so much from Johnson under the stimulus of North Wales and she was chagrined and hurt by his barely concealed dislike of her country. He had frequently been churlish and irritable and not all of this could be ascribed to his health. As she wrote later in her *Anecdotes*: "He was in some respects an admirable Companion on the road as he piqued himself upon feeling no inconvenience, and on despising no accommodations. On the other hand however, he expected no one else to feel any, and felt exceedingly inflamed with anger if anyone complained of the rain, the sun, or the dust. 'How (said he) do other people bear them?'" Again, though Johnson was not insensible to the charms of nature, his primary concern was with human nature. As he later declared, "a blade of grass is always a blade of grass, whether in one country or another: let us, if we do talk, talk about something: men and women are my subjects of enquiry; let us see how these differ from those we have left behind."

At certain times, especially when she was feeling unwell or her companions

---

* A family expression. Agnes was a clinging-vine type of woman in Molière's *L'Ecole des Femmes*.
+ See Johnson Note 26.

were being boorish, she longed for a woman friend to "chat with"; above all, she missed being able to confide in her mother. She had also been upset because she found that "my relations were not quite as forward as I thought they might have been to welcome a long-distant kinswoman", though this could not fairly be applied to the Cottons at Lleweni. Perhaps she failed to appreciate that the prospect of such a curious and sophisticated entourage from London descending upon unsuspecting country houses might not enthuse their owners. Even when relatives and friends did go out of their way to arrange entertainment or visits, these were not always appreciated by the members of the party.

When Johnson arrived back at his house in London, he found letters from Boswell and wrote to him thus on 1st October:

"Yesterday I returned from my Welch journey. I was sorry to leave my book suspended so long; but having an opportunity of seeing, with so much convenience, a new part of the island, I could not reject it. I have been in five of the six Counties of North Wales, and have seen St Asaph and Bangor, the two seats of their bishops; have been upon Penmaenmaur and Snowden, and passed over into Anglesey. But Wales is so little different from England that it offers nothing to the speculation of the traveller."

Boswell commented somewhat tartly:

"This tour to Wales, though it no doubt contributed to his health and amusement, did not give an occasion to such a discursive exercise of his mind as our tour to the Hebrides... All that I heard him say of it was, that 'instead of bleak and barren mountains, there were green and fertile ones; and that one of the castles in Wales would contain all the castles that he had seen in Scotland'."

Reflecting further on his somewhat disappointing excursion, Johnson wrote to John Taylor at Ashbourne on the 20th October in much the same strain:

"Our journey took up more time than we expected, and we did not come to town till the day after the dissolution of the parliament. We entered North Wales from Chester and went to the extremities of Carnavonshire, and passed into Anglesea, and came back by Wrexham and Shrewsbury. But Wales has nothing that can much excite or gratify curiosity. The mode of life is entirely English. I am glad I have seen it, though I have seen nothing because I now know that there is nothing to be seen."

When, three years later, Boswell himself became interested in visiting Wales, Johnson could not hide a rankling disappointment when he wrote to Mrs. Thrale on 13th September, 1777:

"Boswell wants to see Wales; but except the woods of Bachecraig, what is there in Wales, that can fill the hunger of ignorance, or quench the thirst of curiosity?" Duppa commented amusingly that if Johnson had been writing to Boswell instead of Mrs. Thrale he would no doubt have observed that in

Scotland there was little else to make an impression on the traveller but high hills, which, by constantly clouding the view, forced the mind to find entertainment for itself in contemplating hopeless sterility or useless vegetation.

Fortunately, as the months went by, the memory of the friction and the irritations of the tour began to fade. Petty annoyances and minor grievances were forgotten as thoughts turned to a first visit to the Continent. Johnson could contemplate with pleasure the prospect of joining the Thrales on a tour to a country where the mode of life was far from English – or Welsh – and the following summer saw the same party making preparations for the long-awaited tour of France.

A Journey into North Wales in the Year 1774

Samuel Johnson

Samuel Johnson, L.L.D. (by courtesy of the National Library of Wales)

JULY 5, TUESDAY.
11. a.m. We left Streatham.
Price of 4 horses 2s. a mile.
1. p.m. 1.40 Barnet.
At night to Dunstable.
On the road I read Tully's Epistles.[1]

6 [JULY].
To Lichfield 83 miles.
To the Swan.[2]

7 [JULY].
To Mrs. Porters, to the Cathedral. To Mrs. Astons.[3] To Mr. Greens.[4]
Mr. Greens Museum was much admired, and Mr Newton's China.

8 [JULY].
To Mr. Newton's.[5] To Mrs. Cobb.[6]
Dr. Darwin's.[7]
I went again to Mrs. Aston's. She was sorry to part.

9 [JULY].
Breakfast at Mr. Garricks.[8]
Visited Miss Vise.[9] Miss Seward.[10]
Went to Dr. Taylors.[11]
I read a little on the road in Tully's Epistles and Martial.

10 [JULY].
Morning at Church.[12] Company at Dinner.

11 [JULY].
At Ilam.[13] At Okeover.[14]
I was less pleased with Ilam than when I saw it first; but my friends were much delighted.

12 [JULY].
At Chatsworth.[15] The water willow, the Cascade, shot out from many spouts.

The fountains. The water tree. The smooth floors in the highest rooms. Atlas 15 hands inch and half. Surly's Humours.[16] River running through the park. The porticos on the sides, support two galleries for the first floor.

My friends were not struck with the house. It fell below my ideas of the furniture. The Staircase is in the corner of the house. The Hall in the corner the grandest room, though only a room of passage. On the ground floor only the Chappel, and breakfast room, and a small library. The rest servants rooms and offices.

A bad inn.[17]

13 [JULY].
At Matlock.

14 [JULY].
At Dinner, at Oakover[18], too deaf to hear or much converse. Mrs. Gell.[19]

The chapel at Oakover. The wood of the pews grossly painted. I could not read the epitaph. Would learn the old hands.

15 [JULY].
Mart 8, 44. lino pro limo.[20]

At Ashbourne. Mrs. Diot[21] and her daughters came in the morning. Mr. Diot dined with us. We visited Mr. Flint.[22]
Τὸ πρῶτον Μῶρος, τὸ δὲ δεύτερον εἷλεν Ἐρασμὸς,
Τὸ τρίτον εκ Μουσῶν στέμμα Μίκυλλος ἔχει. [23]

16 [JULY].
At Dovedale,[24] with Mr. Langley[25] and Mr. Flint. It is a place that deserves a visit, but did not answer my expectation. The river is small, the rocks are grand. Reynard's hall is a cave very high in the rock, [it] goes backward several yards, perhaps eight. To the left is a small opening through which I crept, and found another cavern perhaps four yards square, at the back was a breach yet smaller, which I could not easily have entered, and, wanting light did not inspect. I was in a cave yet higher called Reynard's kitchen. There is a rock called the Church, in which I saw no resemblance, that could justify the name. Dovedale is about two miles long. We walked towards the head of the Dove which is said to rise about five miles above two caves called the dog holes [Dove-holes], at the end of Dovedale.

In one place where the Rocks approached I propose to build an arch from rock to rock over the stream, with a summerhouse upon it. The water murmured pleasantly among the stones.
I thought that the heat and exercise mended my hearing. I bore the fatigue of the walk, which was very laborious without inconvenience.

There were with us Gilpin[26] and Parker.[27] Having heard of this place before, I had formed some confused idea, to which it did not answer. Brown[28] says he was disappointed. I certainly expected a larger river where I found only a clear quick brook. I believe I had imaged a valley enclosed by rocks, and terminated by a broad expanse of water.

He that has seen Dovedale has no need to visit the Highlands.

In the afternoon we visited old Mrs. Dale.[29]

17 [JULY].
Sunday. Morning at Church.

Afternoon at Mr. Dyot's.
Καθ. [30]

18 [JULY].
Dined at Mr. Gell's.

19 JULY.
We went to Kedleston[31] to see Lord Scarsdales new house, which is very costly but illcontrived. The hall is very stately, lighted by three sky lights; it has two rows of marble pillars dug as I hear from Langley in a quarry of Northamptonshire. The pillars are very large and massy and take up two much room. They were better away. Behind the hall is a circular salon, useless and therefore illcontrived. The corridors that join the wings to the body, are mere passages, through segments of circles. The state bedchamber was very richly furnished. The dining parlour was more splendid with gilt plate than any that I have seen. There were many pictures. The grandeur was all below; the bedchambers were small, low, dark and fitter for a prison than a house of splendour. The Kitchen has an opening into the gallery, by which its heat and its fumes are dispersed over the house. There seemed in the whole more cost than judgement.

We went then to the Silkmil[l] at Derby,[32] where I remarked a particular manner

of propagating motion from a horizontal to a vertical wheel. We were desired to leave the men only two shillings. Mr. Thrales bill at the inn for dinner was 0-18-10 [18s.10d. or 95p].
At night I went to Mr. Langley, Mrs. Wood, Captain Astle,[33] &c.

20 [JULY].
We left Ashbourn, and went to Buxton, thenc[e] to Pool's hole[34] which is narrow at first, but then rises into a high arch, but is so obstructed with crags that it is difficult to walk in it. There are two ways to the end which is, they say six hundred and fifty yards from the mouth. They take passengers up the higher way and bring them back the lower. The higher way was so difficult and dangerous, that having tried it I desisted. I found no level part.

At night we came to Macclesfield[35] a very large town in Cheshire, little known. It has a silk mill. It has a handsome church, which however is but a chapel, for the town belongs to some parish of another name as Stourbridge lately did to Old Swinford. Macclesfield has a town hall and is, I suppose, a corporate town.

21 [JULY].
We came to Congleton, where there is likewise a silk mill.[36] Then to Middlewich a mean old town, without any manufacture, but I think a corporation. Thence we proceeded to Namptwich [Nantwich],[37] an old town, from the Inn, I saw scarcely any but black timber houses. I tasted the brine water, which contains much more salt than the sea-water. By slow evaporation they make large crystals of salt, by quick boiling small granulations. It seemed to have no other preparation.

At evening we came to Combermere,[38] so called from a wide lake.

22 [JULY].
We went upon the Mere. I pulled a bulrush of about ten feet.

23 [JULY].
We visited Lord Kilmurrey's [Kilmorey] house.[39] It is large and convenient, with many rooms, none of which are magnificently spacious. The furniture was not splendid. The bed curtains were guarded.[40] Lord K. showd the place with too much exultation. He has no park, and little water.

24 [JULY].
We went to a Chapel[41] built by Sir Linch Cotton for his Tenants. It is consecrated

and therefore, I suppose, endowed. It is neat and plain. The communion plate is handsome. It has iron pales and gates of great elegance, brought from Llewenny [Lleweni]. "For Robert[42] has laid all open."

25 [JULY].
We saw Hakeston [Hawkstone],[43] the seat of Sir Rowland Hill, and were conducted by Miss Hill over a large tract of rocks and woods, a region abounding with striking scenes and terrifick grandeur. We were always on the brink of a precipice or at the foot of a lofty rock, but the steeps were seldom naked; in many places Oaks of uncommon magnitude shot up from the crannies of stone, and where there were not tall trees, there were underwoods and bushes. Round the rocks is a narrow path, cut upon the stone which is very frequently hewn into steps, but art has proceeded no further than [to] make the succession of wonders safely accessible. The whole circuit is somewhat laborious, it is terminated by a grotto cut in the rock to a great extent with many windings and supported by pillars, not hewn into regularity, but such as imitate the sports of nature, by asperi[ties] and protuberances.

The place is without any dampness, and would afford a habitation not uncomfortable. There were from space to space seats in the rock. Though it wants water it excells Dovedale, by the extent of its prospects, the awfulness of its shades, the horrors of its precipices, the verdure of its hollows and the loftiness of its rocks. The Ideas which it forces upon the mind, are the sublime, the dreadful, and the vast. Above, is inaccessible altitude, below, is horrible profundity. But it excells the Garden of Ilam only in extent.

Ilam has grandeur tempered with softness. The walker congratulates his own arrival at the place, and is grieved to think that he must ever leave it. As he looks up to the rocks his thoughts are elevated; as he turns his eyes on the vallies, he is composed and soothed.

He that mounts the precipices at Hawkeston, wonders how he came hither, and doubts how he shall return. His walk is an adventure and his departure an escape. He has not the tranquility, but the horrour of solitude, a kind of turbulent pleasure between fright and admiration.

Ilam is the fit abode of pastoral virtue, and might properly diffuse its shades over nymphs and swains. Hawkeston can have no fitter inhabitants than Giants of mighty bone, and bold emprise,[44] men of lawless courage and heroic violence. Hawkestone should be described by Milton and Ilam by Parnel.[45]

Miss Hill showed the whole succession of wonders with great civility. The House was magnificent compared with the rank of the owner.

26 [JULY].
We left Cumbermere, where we have been treated with great civility. Sir L. is gross, the Lady weak and ignorant.[46] The House is spacious but not magnificent, built at different times with different materials, part is of timber, part of stone or brick, plaistered and painted to look like timber. It is the best house that I ever saw of that kind.

The Meer or lake is large with a small island, on which there is a summer house shaded with great trees. Some were hollow and have seats in their trunks.

In the afternoon we came to West Chester (my Father went to the fair when I had the small pox). We walked round the walls[47] which are compleat, and contain one Mile, three quarters, and one hundred and one yards[;] within them are many gardens. They are very high, and two may walk very commodiously side by side. On the inside is a rail; there are towers from space to space not very frequent, and I think not all compleat.

27 [JULY].
We staid at Chester and saw the Cathedral,[48] which is not of the first rank. The Castle, in one of the rooms the Assizes are held, and the refectory of the old abbey of which part is a Grammar School. The Master seemed glad to see me. The cloister is very solemn, over it a [re] chambers, in which the singing men live.

In one part of the street was a subterranean arch very strongly built, in another what they called, I believe rightly, a Roman hypocaust.[49]

Chester has many curiosities.

28 [JULY].
We entered Wales, dined at Mold, and came to Llewenny.[50]

29 [JULY].
We were at Llewenny.

[The following paragraphs are entries from 1st August and from Johnson's 'Notes and Omissions' later in his diary.]

A Journey into North Wales in the Year 1774 37

Lleweni Hall in 1789.

N[ote]. In the lawn of Lleweney is a spring of fine water which rises above the surface into a stone basin, from which it runs to waste in a continual stream through a pipe. There are very large trees.
The Hay barn built with brick pillars from space to space, and covered with a roof. A mere elegant and lofty Hovel.

The rivers here are mere torrents which are suddenly swelled by the rain to great breadth and great violence but have very little constant stream. Such are the Clwyd and the Elwas [Elwy]. There are yet no mountains. The ground is beautifully embellished with woods, and diversified by inequalities.

The Hall at Llewenny is 40 feet long and 28 broad. The Gallery 120 feet long (all paced); the Library 42 feet long, and 28 broad. The dining parlour 30 feet long 26 broad.

Ll[ewenny] is partly sashed and partly has casements.

30 [JULY].
We went to Bachycraig[51] where we found an old house built 1567 in an

uncommon and incommodious form. My Mistress chattered about tiring, but I prevailed on her to go to the top. The floors have been stolen; the windows are stopped. The house was less than I seemed to expect.
The River Clwyd is a brook with a bridge of one arch about one third of a mile.

The woods have many trees generally young, but some which seem to decay. They have been lopped. The house never had a garden. The addition of another story would make an useful house, but it cannot be great; some buildings which Clough the founder intended for ware houses would make store-chambers and servants rooms. The ground seems to be good. I wish it well.

31 [JULY].
We went to Church at St. Asaph. The Cathedral though not large has something of dignity and Grandeur. The cross isle is very short. It has scarcely any monuments. The Quire has, I think thirty two stalls,[52] of antique workmanship. On the backs were Canonicus, Prebend, Cancellarius, Thesaurarius, Praecentor. The constitution I do not know but it has all the usual titles and dignities. The service was sung only in the Psalms and hymns.

The Bishop[53] was very civil. We went to his palace, which is but mean. They have a library, and design a room. Here lived Lloyd and Dodwel.[54]

AUGUST 1.
We visited Denbigh and the remains of its Castle.[55] The town consists of one main street, and some that cross it which I have not seen. The chief street ascends with a quick rise for a great length. The houses are built some with rough stone, some with brick, and a few are of timber.

The Castle, with its whole enclosure has been a prodigious pile, it is now so ruined that the form of the inhabited part cannot easily be traced. There are as in all old buildings said to be extensive vaults which the ruins of the upper works cover and conceal but into which boys sometimes find a way. To clear all passages and trace the whole of what remains would require much labour and expence.

We saw a church,[56] which was once the chapel of the castle, but is used by the town, it is dedicated to St. Hilary and has an income of about [amount omitted].

At a small distance is the ruin of [a] Church said to [have] been begun by the great Earl of Leicester,[57] and left unfinished at his death. One side and I think

the East end are yet standing. There was a stone in the wall over the doorway, which it was said, would fall and crush the best scholar in the diocese. One Price would not pass under it. They have taken it down.
We then saw the Chapel of [Lleweni][58], founded by one of the Salusburies. It is very complete, the monumental stones lye in the ground. A chimney has been added to it, but it is otherwise not much injured, and might be easily repaired.

We then went to the parish church of Denbigh[59] which being near a mile from the town is only used when the Parish Officers are chosen.

In the parish Church of Denbigh is a bas relief of Lluyd[60] the antiquary who was before Camden.[61] He is kneeling at his prayers.

In the chapel on Sundays the service is read thrice, the second time only in English, the first and third in Welsh.

The Bishop came to survey the Castle and visited likewise St Hilary's chapel which is that which the town uses.

AUGUST 2.
[I have incorporated here several notes made by Johnson after his entry for August 2nd under *Notes and Omissions*.]

We rode to a summerhouse of Mr. C[otton], which has a very extensive prospect. It is meanly built and unskilfully disposed.

We then went to Dimerchion [Tremeirchion] Ch[urch], where the old Clerk acknowledged his mistress.

The old Clerk had great appearance of joy at the sight of his Mistress, and foolishly said, that he was now willing to die. The old Clerk had only a crown given him by my mistress.[62]

It is the parish Church of Bachycraig, a mean fabrick. Mr. Salusbury was buried in it. Bachicraig has fourteen seats in it.

At Dymerchion Church, the Texts on the walls are in Welsh.

At Dymerchion Church there is English service only once a Month. This is about twenty miles from the English Border.

St. Winifride's Well, Holywell, in 1830.

As we rode by I looked at the house again. We saw Llannerk [Llannerch],[63] a house not mean, with a small park very well watered. There was an avenue of oaks, which in a foolish compliance with the present mode, has been cut down. A few are yet standing. The owner's name is Davies. The way lay through pleasant lanes, and overlooked a region beautifully diversified with trees and grass.

AUGUST 3.
We went in the coach to Holywel[l]. Talk with Mistress about flattery.[64]

Holywel is a Market town neither very small nor mean. The spring called Winifred's Well[65] is very clear, and so copious that it yields one hundred tuns of water in a minute. It is all at once a very great stream which within perhaps thirty yards of its eruption turns a mill and in a course of two miles eighteen mills more. In descent it [is] very quick. It then falls into the sea. The Well is covered by a lofty circular arch supported by pillars, and over this arch is an old Chapel, now a school. The Chancel is separated by a wall. The Bath is completely and indecently open. A Woman bathed while we all looked on.

In the Church,[66] which makes a good appearance, and is surrounded by galleries to receive a numberous congregation, we were present while a child was christened in Welsh.

We went down by the stream to see a prospect in which I had no part. We then saw a brass work[67] where the lapis Calaminaris is gath[e]red, broken, washed from the earth and the lead, though how the lead was separated I did not see, then calcined, afterwards ground fine, and then mixed by fire with the copper.

We saw several strong fires with melting pots, but the construction of the fireplaces I did not learn.

At a copper work, which receives its pigs of copper, I think, from Warrington, we saw a plate of copper put hot between steel rollers, and spread thin. I know not whether [the] upper roller was set to a certain distance, as I suppose, or acted only by its weight.

At an iron work I saw round bars formed by a notched hammer and anvil. Then I saw a bar of about half an inch or more square, cut with sheers worked by water and then beaten hot into a thinner bar; the hammers, all worked as they were by water, acting upon small bodies moved very quick, as quick as by the hand.

I then saw wire drawn, and gave a shilling. I have enlarged my notions. Though not being able to see the movements, and having not time to peep closely, I know less than I might. I was less weary, and had better breath as I walked further.

I had καθ the day before, and had some of the effects this morning.

AUG[UST] 4.
Ruthlan [Rhuddlan] Castle[68] is still a very noble ruin. All the walls still remain so that a compleat platform, and elevations not very imperfect may be taken. It incloses a square of about thirty yards. The middle space was always open. The wall is I believe about thirty feet high very thick, flanked with six round towers each about eighteen feet, or less, in diameter. Only one tower had a chimney, so that here was [little?] commodity of living. It was only a place of strength. The Garrison had perhaps tents in the area.

Stapilton's house [See Thrale Note 36] is pretty[;] there are pleasing shades about it, with a constant spring that supplies a cold bath.
We then went to see a cascade,[69] I trudged unwillingly, and was not sorry to find it dry. The water was however turned on, and produced a very striking cataract. They are paid an hundred pounds a year, for permission to divert the stream to the mines. The River for such it may be termed rises from a single spring, which like that of Winifred is covered with a building.

We called then at another house belonging to Mr. Lloyd which made a handsome appearance.[70] This country seems full of very splendid houses.

Mrs. T[hrale] lost her purse. She expressed so much uneasiness that I concluded the sum to be very great, but when I heard of only seven guineas, I was glad to find she had so much sensibility of money.
I could not drink this day either coffee or tea after dinner. I know not when I missed before.

AUG[UST] 5.
Last night my sleep was remarkably quiet. little flatus.[71] I know not whether by fatigue in walking, or by forbearance of tea. I gave [up] the Ipecacuanha-Vin.Emet had failed, so had tartar Emet. The Ipec. did but little.

I dined at Mr. Middleton's of Gwaynynog.[72] The house was a Gentlemans house below the second rate, perhaps below the third [,] built of stone roughly cut. The rooms were low, and the passage above stairs gloomy, but the furniture was good. The table was well supplied, except that the fruit was bad. It was truly the dinner of a country Gentleman. Two tables were filled with company not inelegant. After dinner the talk was of preserving the Welsh language. I offered them a scheme. Poor Evan Evans[73] was mentioned as incorrigibly addicted to strong drink. Worthington[74] was commended. Middleton is the only man who in Wales has talked to me of literature. I wish he were truly zealous. I recommended the republication of David ap Rhees's Welsh Grammar.[75]

Two sheets of Hebrides came to me for correction to day, F.G.

AUGUST 6.
Καθ[αρσις] δρ[αστικη]. I corrected the two sheets. My sleep last night was disturbed.

Washing at Chester, and here – 5s. 1d.

I did not read. Atterbury's version a heap of barbarity.[76] The Καθ did not much, but I hope, enough.

I saw to day more of the outhouses at Lleuwenny. It is in the whole a very spacious house.

AUGUST 7.
I was at Church at Botfarry [Bodfari]. There was a service used for a sick woman, not canonically, but such as I have heard, I think, formerly at Lichfield, taken out of the visitation. Καθ μετριὼς.

The Church is mean but has a square tower for the bells, rather too stately for the Church.[77]

[AUGUST] 8.
The Bishop and much company dined at Llewenny. Talk of Greek and of the Army. The D[uke] of M[arlborough]s officers useless. Read Phocyllides[78], distinguished the paragraphs.

[AUGUST] 9.
Looked in Leland,[79] an unpleasant book of mere hints. Lichfield School 10 l. and 5 l from the hospital.

[AUGUST] 10.
At Lloyds of Macemunnon [Maesmynnan],[80] a good house, and very large walled garden. I read Windus's Account of his journey to Mequinez, and of Stuarts Embassy.[81] I had read in the Morning Wasse's Greek trochaics to Bentley.[82] They appeared inelegant and made with difficulty. The Latin Elegy contains only common places harshly expressed so far as I have read, for it is long. They seem to be the verses of a Scholar, who has no practice of writing. The Greek I did not always fully understand. I am in doubt about [the] 6th and last paragraphs. Perhaps they are not printed right; for εὔτοκον perhaps εὔστοχον. q.

The following days I read here and there. The Bibl. Literaria, was so little supplied with papers that could interest curiosity, tha[t] it could not hope for long continuance. Wasse the chief contributor was an unpolished Scholar, who with much literature, had no art or elegance of diction, at least in English.

[AUGUST 11.]
No entry.

[AUGUST 12.]
No entry.

[AUGUST 13.]
No entry.

AUGUST 14.
At Botfarry I heard the second Lesson read, and the sermon preached in Welsh. The text was pronounced both in Welsh and English. The sound of the Welsh in a continued discourse is not unpleasant.

Βρῶσις ὀλίγη Καθ[αρσις] α[νευ] φ[αρμακων] [83]

The Letter of Chrysostom against transubstantiation. Erasmus to the Nuns, full of mystick notions, and allegories.[84]

AUG[UST] 15.
Καθ. Imbecillitas genuum non sine aliquantulo doloris inter ambulandum, quem a prandio magis sensi.[85]

[AUGUST 16.]
No entry; [but on that day he wrote to his friend, Robert Levet,[86] as follows:

Dear Sir,
  Mr. Thrale's affairs have kept him here a great while, nor do I know exactly when we shall come hence. I have sent you a bill upon Mr. Strahan.
  I have made nothing of the ipecacuanha, but have taken abundance of pills, and hope that they have done me good.
  Wales, so far as I have yet seen of it, is a very beautiful and rich country, all enclosed and planted. Denbigh is not a mean town. Make my Compliments to all my friends and tell Frank I hope he remembers my advice. When his money is out, let him have more. I am, Sir,

Your humble servant,

Sam. Johnson.]

[AUGUST 17.]
No entry.

AUG[UST] 18.
We left Llewenni, and went forwards on our Journey. We came to Abergeler [Abergele] a mean town in which little but Welsh is spoken, and Divine Service is seldom performed in English. Our way then lay by the sea side, at the foot of a Mountain called Penman ross [Penmaen Rhos]. Here the way was so steep that we walked on the lower edge of the hill to meet the Coach that went upon a road higher on the hill. Our walk was not long nor unpleasant, the longer I walk the less I feel its inconvenience. As I grow warm my breath mends and I think my limbs grow pliable.

We then came to Conway Ferry, and passed in small boats, with some passengers from the Stage coach, Among whom were an Irish Gentlewoman with two maids and three little children of which the youngest was only a few months old. The tide did not serve the large ferry boat, and therefore our Coach could not very soon follow us. We were therefore to stay at the Inn. It is now the day of the race at Conway[87] and the town was so full of company, that no money could purchase lodging. We were not very readily supplied with cold dinner. We would have stayed at Conway, if we could have found entertainment, for we were afraid of passing Penmanmawr [Penmaenmawr] over which lay our way to Bangor but by bright daylight, and the delay of our coach made our departure necessarily late. There was however no stay on any other terms than of sitting up all night.

The poor Irish Lady was still more distressed. Her children wanted rest. She would have been content with one bed, but for a time none could be had. Mrs. T[hrale] gave her what help she could. At last two gentlemen were persuaded to yield up their room with two beds, for which she gave half a guinea.

Our coach was at last brought and we set out with some anxiety but we came to Penmanmawr by day light, and found a way lately made very easy and very safe.[88] It was cut smooth and inclosed between parallel walls. The outer of which secures the [traveller?] from the precipice which is deep and dreadful. This wall is here and there broken by mischievous wantonness. The inner wall preserves the road from the loose stones which the shatter[ed] steeps above it would pour down. That side of the mountain seems to have a surface of loose stones which every accident may crumble. The old road was higher and must have been very formidable. The sea beats at the bottom of the way. At Evening the Moon shone eminently bright, and our thoughts of danger being now past, the rest of our journey was very pleasant. At an hour somewhat late we came to Bangor, where we found a very mean Inn, and had some difficulty to obtain lodging. I lay in a room where the other bed had two men. I had a flatulent night.

AUGUST 19.
We obtained a boat to convey us to Anglesea [Anglesey], and saw Lord Bulkley's [Bulkeley] house[89] and Beaumaris Castle.[90] I was accosted by Mr Lloyd the Schoolmaster of Beaumaris[91] who had seen me at University College and he with Mr. Roberts the Register of Bangor[92] whose boat we borrowed, accompanied us. Lord Bulkeley's house is very mean, but his garden is spacious and shady, with large trees and smaller interspersed. The walks are strait and cross each other with no variety of plan but they have a pleasing coolness and solemn gloom, and extend to a great length.

The Castle is a mighty pile[:] the outward wall has fifteen round towers, besides square towers at the angles. There is then a void space between the wall and the castle, which has an area enclosed with a wall which again has towers larger than those of the outer wall; the towers of the inner castle are I think eight. There is likewise a chapel entire, bui[l]t upon an arch as I suppose, and beautifully arch[ed] with a stone roof which is yet unbroken. The entrance into the Chapel is about eight or nine feet high, and was I suppose, higher when there was no rubbish in the area.

This castle corresponds with all the representations of romancing narratives.

The Headmaster's House and remains of the old Grammar School, Beaumaris.

Here is not wanting the private passage, the dark cavity, the deep dungeon or the lofty tower. We did not discover the well. This is [the] most complete view that I have yet had of an old castle. It had a moat.
The towers.

We returned to Bangor.

AUGUST 20.
We went by water from Bangor to Caernarvon,[93] where we met Poali [Paoli][94] and Sir Thomas Wynne.[95] Meeting by chance with one Troughton,[96] an intelligent and loquacious wanderer, Mr. T[hrale] invited him to din[n]er. He attended us to the Castle, an Edifice of stupendous magnitude and strength. It has in it all that we observed at Beaumaris, [but?] of much greater dimensions; many of the smaller rooms floored with stone are entire; of the larger rooms, the beams and planks are all lost; this is [the] state of all buildings left to time. We mounted the Eagle tower by 169 steps each of ten inches. We did not find the well, nor did I trace the moat, but moats there were I believe to all castles on the plain, which not only hindred access, but prevented mines. We saw but a very small part of this mighty ruin. And in all these old buildings, the subterraneous works are concealed by the rubbish. To survey this place would take much time. I did not think there had been such buildings. It surpassed my Ideas.

[AUGUST] 21.
We were at Church, the service in the town is always English, at the Parish Church at a small distance always Welsh.[97] The town has by degrees, I suppose, been brought nearer to the sea side. We received an invitation to Dr Worthington. We then went to din[n]er at Sir T. Wynne's. The Dinner mean, Sir T. civil. His Lady nothing.[98] Poali civil.

We supped with Colonel Wynne's Lady[99] who lives in one of the towers of the Castle.

I have not been very well.

AUGUST 22.
We went to visit Bodville [Bodfel], the place where Mrs. T[hrale] was born, and the churches called Tydweilliog [Tydweiliog] and Llangynnidle [Llangwnnadl] which she holds by impropriation.[100] We had an invitation to the House of Mr Griffith of Brinoddle [Brynodol], where we found a small neat new built house with square rooms. The walls are of unhewn stone and therefore thick, for the

Caernarfon Castle in the 19th century. The Eagle Tower can be seen on the extreme left.

stones not fitting with exactness are not strong without great thickness. He had planted a great deal of young wood in walks. Fruit trees do not thrive, but having grown a few years reach some barren stratum and wither.

We found Mr Griffith not at home, but the provisions were good. Mr. Griffith came home the next day. He married a Lady who has a house and estate at [Llanfairisgaer], over against Anglesea, and near Caernarvon, where she is more disposed, as it seems, to reside than at Brinodl [See Thrale Note 49]

I read Lluyds account of Mona[101] which he proves to be Anglesea. In our way to Br[ynodol], we saw at Llanerk [Clynnog][102] a Church built crosswise very spacious and magnificent for this country; we could not see the Parson and could get no intelligence about it.

[There is no entry for 23 August. In his entry for the 24th Johnson has combined accounts of their visits for both the 23rd and 24th August. In the light of Mrs. Thrale's detailed diary for this period, I have re-arranged this entry to cover their activities on 23 and 24 August.]

[AUGUST 23.]
We went to see Bodvil. Mrs. T[hrale] remembered the rooms, and wandred over them, with recollection of her childhood. This species of pleasure is always

melancholy. The walk was cut down, and the pond was dry. Nothing was better. Mrs. Thrale visited a house where she had been used to drink milk, which was left with an estate of 200 l [pounds] a year, by one Lloyd to a married woman who lived with him.

We went to Pwlhely [Pwllheli] a mean old town at the extremity of the country. Here we bought something to remember the place.

[AUGUST 24.]
We surveyed the churches, which are mean and neglected to a degree scarcely imaginable. They have no pavement, and the earth is full of holes, the seats are rude benches. The altars have no rails; one of them has a breach in the roof. On the desk I think of each lay a Folio Welsh Bible of the black letter, which the Curate cannot easily read. Mr. T[hrale] proposes to beautify the Churches, and, if he prospers, will probably restore the tithes. The two parishes are Llangynnidle and Tydweilliog. The Methodists are here very prevalent. A better church will impress the people with more reverence of publick Worship.

[I have transferred the following note from Johnson's entry for 29 August. Johnson made a small slip: the party did not go to Cefnamwlch on the day they visited Bodvel Hall (23rd) but on the 24th.]

N[ote]. On the day when we visited Bodvil, we turned to the house of Mr. Griffith, of Kefnamwyllch [Cefnamwlch][1],[103] a gentleman of large fortune, remarkable for having made great and sudden improvements, in his seat and estate. He has enclosed a large Garden with a brick wall. He is considered as a Man of great accomplishments. He was educated in literature at the University, and served some time in the army, then quitted his commission, and retired to his Lands. He is accounted a good Man and endeavours to bring the people to church.

[AUGUST] 25.
We returned to Carnarvon where we eat with Mrs. Wynne.

[AUGUST] 26.
We visited with Mrs. Wynne Llyn Badarn [Padarn] and Llyn Beris [Peris], two lakes joined by a narrow strait. They are formed by the waters which fall from Snowden [Snowdon] and the opposite Mountains. On the side of Snowden are the remains of a large fort,[104] to which we climbed with great labour. I was breathless and harrassed. The lakes have no great breadth so that the boat is

Dolbadarn Castle.

always near one bank or the other.
Queeney's Goats 149, I think.[105]

[AUGUST] 27.
We returned to Bangor where Mr. T[hrale] was lodged at Mr. Roberts the Register.

[AUGUST] 28.
We went to worship at the Cathedral. The Quire is mean, the service was not well read.

[AUGUST] 29.
We came to Mr. Middleton's of Gyuannog. To the first place as my Mistress observed, where we have been welcome.

In our way from Bangor to Conway, we passed again the new road upon the edge of Penmanmaur, which would be very tremendous but that the wall shuts out the idea of danger. In the wall are several breaches made as Mr. T[hrale] very reasonably conjectures, by fragments of rocks which roll down the mountain, broken perhaps by frost, or worn through by rain.

We then viewed Conway.[106]

To spare the horses at Penman Ross, between Conway and St. Asaph we sent the coach over the road cross the Mountain, with Mrs. Th[rale] who had been tired with a walk some time before, and I with Mr Th[rale] and Miss, walked along the edge where the path is very narrow, and much encumbred by little loose stones which had fallen down as we thought upon the way since we passed it before.

At Conway we took a short survey of the Castle, which afforded us nothing new. It is larger than that of Beumarris, and less than that of Caernarvon. It is built upon a rock so high and steep that it is even now very difficult of access. We found a round pit which was called the well, it is now almost filled and therefore dry. We found the well in no other castle. There are some remains of leaden pipes at Caernarvon, which, I suppose only conveyed water from one part of the building to another. Had the Garrison had no other supply, the Welsh who must know where the pipes were laid could easily have cut them.

AUG[UST] 29.
We came to the house of Mr. Middleton[107] (on Monday) where we staid to Sept. 6, and were very kindly entertained.

The Cathedral Church of St. Deiniol at Bangor in the early 19th century.

How we spent our time I am not very able to tell. We saw the wood which is diversified and romantick.

[AUGUST 30.]
No entry.

[AUGUST 31.]
No entry.

[SEPTEMBER 1.]
No entry.

[SEPTEMBER 2.]
No entry.

[SEPTEMBER 3.]
No entry.

SEPT[EMBER] 4, SUNDAY.
We dined with Mr Middleton the Clergyman at Denbigh,[108] where I saw the Harvestmen very decently dressed after the afternoon service standing to be hired. On other days they stand at about four in the morning. They are hired from day to day.

[SEPTEMBER 5.]
No entry.

SEPT[EMBER] 6, TUESDAY.
We lay at Wrexham, a busy, extensive and well-built town. It has a very large and magnificent Church.[109] It has a famous fair.

SEPT[EMBER] 7.
We came to Chirk Castle.[110 & 111]

SEPT[EMBER] 8, THURSDAY.
We came to the House of Dr Worthington[112] at Llanrhaiadur [Llanrhaiadr-ym-Mochnant]. Our entertainment was poor though his house was not bad. The Situation is very pleasant by the side of a small river, of which the bank rises high on the other side shaded by gradual rows of trees. The gloom, the stream, and the silence generate thoughtfulness.

The Parish Church of St. Giles, Wrexham.

The town is old and very mean, but has, I think, a market.[113] In this house the Welsh translation of the old testament was made.

The Welsh Singing Psalms were written by Archdeacon Price. They are not considered as elegant, but as very literal and accurate.

We came to Llanrhaiadur through Oswestry, a town not very little nor very mean. The Church[114] which I saw only at a distance seems to be an edifice much too grand for the present state of the place.

SEPT[EMBER] 9.
We visited the Waterfal[115] which is very high, and in rainy weather very copious. There is a reservoir made to supply it. In its fall it has perforated a rock. There is a room built for entertainment. There was some difficulty in climbing to a near view. Lord Littleton came near it, and turned back.

When we came back we took some cold meat, and notwithstanding the D[octo]r's importunities went that day to Shrewsbury.

SEPT[EMBER] 10.
I sent for Gwin,[116] and he showed us the town. The walls are broken, and narrower than those of Chester. The town is large and has many Gentlemens houses, but the streets are narrow. I saw Taylors library.[117] We walked in the Quarry[118], a very pleasant walk by the river. Our inn was not bad.

SEPT[EMBER] 11, SUNDAY.
We were at St. Chads, a very large and luminous Church.[119] We were on the Castle hill.

[SEPTEMBER] 12.
We called on Dr. Adams,[120] and travelled towards Worcester through Wenlock, a very mean place though a borough. At noon we came to Bridgenorth, and walked about the town, of which one part stands on a high rock and part very low by the river. There is an old tower[121] which being crooked leans so much that it is frightful to pass by it.

In the afternoon we went through Kinver a town in Staffordshire, neat and closely built. I believe it has only one street.

The Road was so steep and miry, that we were forced to stop at Hartlebury, where we had a very neat inn, though it made a very poor appearance.

SEPT[EMBER] 13.
We came to Lord Sandys[122] at Ombersley where we were treated with great civility. The house is large. The Hall is a very noble room.

[SEPTEMBER] 14.
We went to Worcester a very splendid city. The Cathedral is very noble with many remarkable monuments. The Library is in the Chapter house, on the table lay the Nuremburg Chronicle, I think, of the first Edition.[123] We went to the China Warehouse. The Cathedral has a cloister. The long isle is in my opinion neither so wide nor so high as that of Lichfield.

[SEPTEMBER] 15.
No entry.

[SEPTEMBER] 16.
We went to Hagley,[124] where we were disappointed of the respect and kindness that we expected.

[SEPTEMBER] 17.
We saw the house and park[125] which equalled my expectation. The house is one square mass. The offices are below. The rooms of elegance on the first floor with two stories of bed Chambers very well disposed above it. The Bedchambers have low windows which abates the dignity of the house.

The park has an artificial ruin, and wants water. There is however one temporary cascade. From the farthest hill there is a very wide prospect.

[SEPTEMBER] 18.
I went to Church. The Church is externally very mean, and is therefore diligently hidden by a plantation. There are in it several modern monuments of the Littletons.[126]

The[re] dined with us, Lord Dudley[127], and Sir [Edward] Littleton[128] of Staffordshire and His Lady, they were all persons of agreeable conversation.

I found time to reflect on my Birthday, and offered a prayer which I hope, was heard.

SEPT[EMBER] 19.
We made haste away from a place where all were offended. In the way we visited the Leasires.[129] It was rain[ing], yet we visited all the waterfalls; there are in one place fourteen falls in a short line. It is the next place to Ilam Garden. Poor Shenstone never tasted his pension. It is not very well proved that any pension was obtained for him. I am afraid that he died of misery.

We came to Birmingham and I sent for Hector,[130] whom I found well.

[SEPTEMBER] 20.
We breakfasted with Hector and visited the Manufacture of Papier mache.[131] The paper which the[y] use is smooth whited brown; the varnish is polished with rotten stone.[132] Hector gave me a tea board. We then went to Boltons,[133] who with great civility led us through his shops. I could not [d]istinctly see his enginery.

Twelve dozen of Buttons for three [s]hillings. Spoons struck at once.

[SEPTEMBER] 21.
Hector came to us again. We came easily to Woodstock.

[SEPTEMBER] 22.
We saw Blenheim and Woodstock park.[134] The park contains 2500 Acres about four square miles. It has red deer.

Mr. Bryant[135] shewed me the Library with great civility. Durandi Rationale. 1459. Lascaris Grammar of the first edition, well printed, but much less than latter Editions. The first Batrachomyomachia.

The Duke sent Mr. Thrale Partridges and fruit. At night we came to Oxford.

[SEPTEMBER] 23.
We visited Mr. Colson.[136] The Ladies wandred about the University.

[SEPTEMBER] 24.
Καθ. We dine with Mr. Colson.

[SEPTEMBER 25]
Van Sittaert[137] told me his distemper.

Afterwards we were at Burke's,[138] where we heard of the dissolution of the parliament. We went home.

Notes on Johnson's Diary

N.B. Johnson and Mrs. Thrale frequently, and naturally, mention the same place, the same person and the same event in their daily diary entries. When such references need to be explained or commented upon, I have, to avoid duplication, taken Johnson first.

1. The letters of Marcus Tullius Cicero, the great Roman orator, writer and statesman.

2. *The Swan Hotel* in Bird Street is not much changed externally from Johnson's day. Although it seemed to have fallen upon evil times several years ago, it is now happily restored.

3. Miss Lucy Porter was Johnson's step-daughter who lived at Redcourt House (now demolished) at the top of Tamworth Street. Miss Elizabeth Aston lived in Stowe Hill, a very handsome Georgian house built about 1754, standing on rising ground beyond St. Michael's Church. The house is in private hands today.

4. Richard Green was an apothecary who had built up a cabinet of curiosities. He had all the articles properly arranged and labelled and a printed catalogue was available. On seeing his small museum Johnson commented, "Sir, I should as soon thought of building a man-of-war as collecting such a museum."

5. Andrew Newton was a wine-merchant in Lichfield and a generous benefactor to his city.

6. Johnson frequently visited the widow, Mrs. Thomas Cobb (he called her "Moll" Cobb) and her niece, Miss Mary Adey, at their home, the Friary. Originally founded by the Franciscans or Grey Friars about 1229, the convent was converted in 1545 into an interesting old mansion standing in grounds of some eleven acres. Much of the house has now been incorporated into Lichfield College which stands by the St. John Street traffic lights.

7. Dr. Erasmus Darwin, grandfather of Charles Darwin, was a doctor in Lichfield and published some poetry stemming from the botanical garden he established in 1778. He and Johnson enjoyed a mutual antipathy. His splendid house still stands in Beacon Street.

8. This was Peter, David Garrick's elder brother. Boswell found him "strongly resembling him in countenance and voice, but of more sedate and placid manners ... " and Johnson thought that David's vivacity was not so peculiar to himself as was supposed. "Sir, (said he,) I don't know but if Peter had cultivated all the arts of gaiety as much as David has done, he might have been as brisk and lively. Depend upon it, Sir, vivacity is much an art, and depends greatly on habit."

9. Miss Mary Vyse, daughter of the Rev. W. Vyse, archdeacon of Shropshire.

10. Anna Seward (1747-1809), poet, was known as "The Swan of Lichfield". She did not much care for Johnson and Mrs. Piozzi noted that "Dr. Johnson would not suffer me to speak to Miss Seward."

11. The Rev. John Taylor figures prominently in Johnson's life. He was at school at Lichfield with Johnson and they remained close friends all their lives. Inheriting a large estate, he became Rector of Market Bosworth by purchase, and was also one of the Duke of Devonshire's chaplains. Taylor was typical of the wealthy 18th c. "dignified" divine (Boswell later described him as "a hearty English 'Squire', with the parson super-induced.") and Johnson frequently visited him. He was a generous host to the party for the next eleven days. He lived opposite the Grammar School in Church Street in a house known as the Mansion, which was built in 1685 on the site of a chantry priest's house. In 1761-63 it was considerably altered by Robert Adam, the facade being refronted and an octagonal domed drawing room added. Today the Mansion is the boarding house for girls attending the co-educational Grammar School opposite and behind the somewhat dingy facade lurks a restored interior of great charm. The unexpectedly large garden is most attractive with an arbour, an extensive lawn and a pond (alas, no waterfall) among the trees at the bottom.

12. They attended the mediaeval church of St. Oswald's a few yards from Dr. Taylor's house. George Eliot described it as "the finest mere parish church in the kingdom." I could not trace Dr. Taylor's "magnificent seat" referred to by Mrs. Thrale. Dr. Taylor was almost certainly buried in a vault in the south transept, but when the vault was filled in in 1884 his body was re-interred in the churchyard outside the south door in a bricked tomb covered with a stone slab. There is no inscription on the slab.

13. See Thrale Note 15.

14. See Johnson Note 18.

15. Chatsworth, one of the greatest country houses in England, was the seat of the Dukes of Devonshire. Today it is very different from the house Johnson saw. The Elizabethan house built in 1555 by Bess of Hardwick was obliterated by the re-building carried out by William Cavendish, the 1st Duke, between 1686 and 1707. Then, between 1755 and 1763, the 4th Duke made further alterations and employed Capability Brown to landscape his parkland of some 1,000 acres. This is the house the party saw. At this time the Painted Hall, which Johnson admired, was still floored with gritstone slabs, the marble pavement not being laid until 1779. During the 1820s the 6th Duke made considerable additions and the whole of the present approach – the lodges and entrance gates, the drive and the north wing on the left, dominated by the theatre tower – stem from this period. The gardens, which cover one hundred acres, were famous for the Great Cascade and several fountains, among them the charming Willow Tree fountain which Mrs. Piozzi described as "a water-work with a concealed spring which, upon touching, spouted out streams from every bough of a willow tree." It is strange to read Johnson's and Mrs. Thrale's less than enthusiastic comments on a house which is rightly known today as "the Palace of the Peak".

16. Atlas was a handsome, famous race-horse to which Johnson took such a fancy that he declared, "of all the Duke's possessions, I like Atlas best." Surley was another of the Duke's horses.

17. This was almost certainly a house in the upper part of Edensor on the west side of the green. Arthur Young, who stayed there a few years earlier, warned the traveller in his *Farmer's Tour through the East of England* (1771), "he will find here nothing but dirt and impertinence."

18. Johnson's host was Edward Okeover, formerly Edward Walhouse, who had assumed the name of Okeover when he inherited the estate at the death of his great uncle, Loake Okeover, in 1763. The "chapel" at Okeover used to be the parish church and was thoroughly restored by Sir Gilbert Scott in 1859. The epitaph which Johnson could not read was that originally inscribed to the memory of William, Lord Zouch, who died in 1447, but altered to commemorate Humphrey Okeover, who died in 1538. (See Mrs. Thrale's racy comment on her visit to the chapel on 14th July.) Today the Hall is the home of Sir Peter Walker-Okeover, and neither the Hall nor the church is open to the public.

19. Philip Gell of Hopton Hall, Sheriff of Derbyshire in 1755, had recently married a young girl of sixteen. The party dined and spent the day with him and his new bride on 18th July. In 1989 the contents of this Elizabethan and Georgian house were auctioned and the estate sold. It had been the home of the Gells, variously soldiers, poets, MPs, and admirals for 600 years.

20. Marcus Valerius Martialis, c.AD 40-104, poet and satirist. The printer obviously put "lino" in the line from Martial's *Eighth Book of Epigrams*: "Defluat, et lento splendescat turbida limo", which Johnson was reading. Johnson commented in his MS: "There seem to be few books less depraved by translation than Martial."

21. Richard Dyott, of Freeford Hall, near Lichfield, was a member of a wealthy Staffordshire family. He and his wife, Catherine, had three sons and four daughters, one of whom married Robert Dale of Ashbourne.

22. Thomas Flint was Dr. Taylor's confidential clerk and aide. In 1766 he married a widow, Mary Collier (née Dunn), who was claimed by Johnson as his "cousin". She died in 1776, leaving two daughters by her first husband and a son and daughter by Flint.

23. "From the Muses, Sir Thomas More bore away the first crown, Erasmus the Second, and Micyllus has the third." The learned Jacob Moltzer (1503-58) took the name Micyllus from the Dialogues of Lucian.

24. The party, like most visitors, walked up the Dale from Thorpe Cloud. To reach Reynard's Cave and Kitchen they had a fairly strenuous scramble up the hillside to the right of the path. They climbed through the great limestone arch and up to the main cave and to the Kitchen beyond it, Johnson exploring it thoroughly. The view of the wooded hill opposite back through the arch is still as attractive as Mrs. Thrale found it. A little way beyond Reynard's Cave the rock walls suddenly close in ("the Streights") and it was here that Johnson imagined building a summer house upon an arch joining the two hillsides. Today there is a boarded walkway along this narrow stretch of the Dove. I have not been able to identify the rock Johnson referred to as the "Church", although there is a large crag on the Staffordshire bank below Ilam Rock which an imaginative eye could take for a tower with a suspicion of a bare ruin'd choir attached to one side of it. The Dove Holes are two huge water-carved hollows marking the end of this beautiful and spectacular section of the Dale.

25. The Rev. William Langley was the quarrelsome and difficult headmaster of Ashbourne Grammar School. Dr. Taylor disliked him intensely and this may account for his being "particularly engaged" on the day of this excursion.

26. This was probably William Gilpin (1757-1848), an Oxford undergraduate and the son of the Reverend William Gilpin [See Johnson Note 125]. He was much smitten with the child Queeney and determined on his return to get his father to seek her hand in marriage for him. They lost no time in doing so but were unsuccessful.

27. John Parker of Browsholme Hall, Clitheroe, who was up at Cambridge; later MP for Clitheroe.

28. Mrs. Piozzi "rather thought this was 'Capability' Brown'" – so called because of his belief that places were "capable of improvement".

29. This was either the mother or grandmother of Robert Dale [See Johnson Note 21].

30. When Johnson wishes to say something in his Diary about his health, he comments in Greek or Latin - perhaps out of a rather surprising delicacy. He had trouble with his bowels and his usual entry is Καθαρσις, abbreviated to Καθ, meaning here a bowel motion. Occasional elaborations are:

> Καθαρσις μετριώς: a moderate motion; and
> Καθαρσις δρ(αστική): apparently a convulsive evacuation.

31. Kedleston House is a Palladian mansion built by Robert Adam for Nathanial Curzon, 1st. Baron Scarsdale, in 1759-65. The house has the most complete and least altered sequence of Adam interiors in England; the rooms still contain their original collection of family portraits and old masters, and also much of the original furniture. The design of the impressive new pile was obviously not to Johnson's taste, though it is surprising that he was not affected by the splendid Saloon with its Pantheon-based, domed rotunda. Actually he and Mrs. Thrale saw the cold magnificence of the Marble Hall before it was altered in 1776-77 to relieve its austerity. On a later visit with Boswell, Johnson remarked that, "It would do excellently well for a Town Hall, the large room with the pillars would do for the Judges to sit in at the assizes, the circular room for a jury chamber, and the room above for prisoners." Langley, incidentally, was wrong about the pillars; they are of veined alabaster from the Redhill quarries in

Nottinghamshire, which also belonged to Lord Scarsdale.

32. This was the first modern silk mill and deservedly famous. The Derby engineer, George Sorocold, built a five-storey, water-powered, silk spinning mill for John and Thomas Lombe in 1717-21 off Full Street on the River Derwent. The mill employed about three hundred people operating machines of much improved design and it provided the model for the textile factories of the Industrial Revolution. The top three floors were used for processing the raw silk imported from Italy, China and India, and the lower ones for weaving. The mill was badly damaged by fire in 1910 and had to be largely rebuilt, but with three high storeys instead of five shallow ones. Some of the original stone foundation arches are still visible on the river front. The mill was re-opened in 1974 as the Derby Industrial Museum with the emphasis very much on Rolls Royce aero-engines and the Midland Railway.

33. Capt. Astle later resigned his Commission in 1778 and took holy orders; Mrs. Wood was his sister, Mary.

34. Poole's Cavern, traditionally named after a 15th c. outlaw who used it as his base, is an open-ended cave lying beneath the wooded slopes of Grin Low and has been an attraction since mediaeval times. The cavern is some 1,000 feet in length, which is at odds with Johnson's comment that "they say" the end is six hundred and fifty yards from the mouth. In Johnson's day, visitors had to scramble some twenty yards through a low and narrow entrance, which opened into a lofty arched area, now referred to as the "Roman Chamber". Then, carrying candles and accompanied by a guide, they clambered up a steep, rugged path to the end of the cavern and back, according to Johnson, along a lower way. Guided parties today follow a firm, sloping path with occasional steps and a bridge to the boulder-choked end, and return the same way. However, up on the right side of the cavern one can trace sections of what might have once been a difficult path. It must certainly have appeared dangerous to deter such an intrepid and indefatigable sight-seer as Johnson. There is an excellent, literate guide-book available.

35. Macclesfield was the centre of the silk trade in this region of the Pennines. Although there were already several silk mills in the town at the time of Johnson's visit, the party almost certainly visited the first water-powered mill which had been built by Charles Roe in 1743. Macclesfield has a fascinating Silk Museum housed in the splendid Sunday School (built 1813) in Roe Street

and there is now a Silk Trail for visitors which includes mills, another museum, and weavers' garrets.

The handsome church was St. Michael and All Angels, the parish church of Macclesfield, which at that time belonged to the parish of Prestbury.

Johnson saw the original Guild Hall, an attractive late 16th c. stone building with gables and latticed, mullioned windows, and three arches on the south side. A double flight of steps led up to the main door. It stood on the site of the present Magistrates Court.

36. Johnson could hardly have missed Pattinson and Clayton's huge mill on the left as his coach crossed the bridge over the River Dane into Congleton. The Old Mill, as it was always known, was five storeys high and long and narrow to maximise the light, and its setting on the north bank of the river against the green backcloth of the Town Wood was most impressive. It was the first mill to be established in the town (1755) and it employed 400 people, sending silk yarn to Spitalfields in London to be woven. Today only the lower two storeys remain.

37. Nantwich (from Nant = valley and wyche or wich = salt pit) was known as Namptwych in the eighteenth century and was the centre of the salt industry in Cheshire. The Romans first discovered the brine pit or salt spring, which is still there by the bridge over the River Weaver and is used today to supply the nearby Brine Swimming Pool. Water from it was conveyed along wooden channels and poured into large lead vats, under which fires were lit to produce salt by evaporation. As Johnson observed, the size of the crystals could be varied by altering the rate of evaporation. When Johnson and the Thrales passed through the town, salt-works covered tracts of land on both sides of the river. The industry began to decline when serious mining of rock salt started at Northwich in 1781, where the economic advantages generated by the new canals in the area proved decisive.

38. Combermere Abbey was the seat of Sir Lynch Salusbury Cotton, Mrs. Thrale's uncle. The house stands by the side of a lake on the site of a 12th c. Cistercian monastery and is not open to the public. There are various monuments to the Cotton family in nearby Wrenbury church.

39. Shavington Hall in Shropshire, home of John Needham, 10th Viscount Kilmorey. John (Jack) Needham had been an officer in the 2nd Foot Guards from 1737 to 1748 and succeeded to the peerage on the death of his father in 1768. He is remembered by a monument, hardly more than a tablet, with a brief

Latin inscription, high up on the north wall of the old chancel in that part of St. Peter's Church, Adderley, which was vested in the Redundant Churches Fund in 1977. See Mrs. Thrale's comments on him. Shavington Hall was pulled down some years ago; only the fine old stables remain and they are in a parlous state.

40. Guarded = trimmed with lace or having an ornamental border. Cf *The Merchant of Venice*, Act II, Scene 2:
Bassanio: (to a servant) Give him a livery more guarded than his fellows.

41. Because the oratory at Combermere proved too small, Sir Lynch built the chapel at Burleydam which was consecrated in 1769. The chapel, though much altered, is still plain and has lost its elegant gates. It is now the church of St. Mary the Virgin and St. Michael and the parish church of Burleydam.

42. Robert, the eldest son of Sir Lynch Cotton and Mrs. Thrale's cousin, lived at Lleweni. This remark, according to some authorities, probably refers to Robert's decision, in the fashion of the time, to level part or all of the walls enclosing his estate, thus making his gates redundant. I find this hard to credit. He might, however, have chosen to remove a pair of gates from an entrance to the house.

43. Hawkstone Park, near Hodnet, Shropshire, remained the seat of the Hill family until 1906. Sir Rowland Hill was formerly the MP for Lichfield (1734-41); his namesake, the founder of the Penny Post, claimed a common origin with the Hills of Hawkstone. Both Mrs. Thrale and Johnson were mightily impressed by the romantic splendours and the rugged grandeur of Hawkestone, as evidenced by the length of their diary entries. They admired the Grotto and the other ornamental buildings, carefully positioned to enhance superb views of the estate and surrounding countryside. The cliffs, rocks, and woods of Hawkstone remain virtually unchanged and unspoilt though the estate now harbours a well-known golf club. Hawkstone Hall itself is today a Redemptionist Pastoral Centre which is open to the public on most afternoons in August.

44. Enterprise. "Giants of mighty bone, and bold emprise:" Milton: Paradise Lost, Book XI, 1.642.

45. Thomas Parnell (1679-1718), a minor Irish poet, friend of Swift and Pope. Johnson wrote a brief life of him in his *Lives of the Poets*, based mainly on a recent and longer work by Goldsmith.

46. Sir Lynch and Lady Cotton were nearly seventy; despite their efforts to

entertain the party, their rustic manners displeased Johnson as much as they had formerly embarrassed their niece.

47. Mrs. Piozzi later wrote to Duppa:

"Of those *ill-fated* walls Dr. Johnson might have learned the extent from any one. He has since put me fairly out of countenance by saying, 'I have known *my mistress* fifteen years, and never saw her fairly out of humour but on Chester wall.' It was because he would keep Miss Thrale beyond her hour of going to bed to walk on the wall, where, from the want of light, I apprehended some accident to her – perhaps to him."

It seems that Johnson was also out of humour at Chester for it was here that he rebuked Mrs. Thrale for what she describes as "a foolborn jest": "Oh, madam, you had rather crack a Joke, I know, than stop to learn any thing I can teach; so take the road you were born to run." [See Thrale Note 27]

48. The refectory of Chester Cathedral was used as a schoolroom for many years by the King's School, founded by Henry VIII. In the nineteenth century the school was transferred to premises on the south side of Abbey Square now occupied by Barclays Bank. In 1960 the school finally moved out of the town centre to new buildings on a greenfield site on the Wrexham Road. The headmaster referred to was the Reverend Richard Vanbrugh.

Because of extensive re-building of the Cathedral, nothing remains of the chambers or Dormitory for the singing men. The Dormitory, according to Bennett's "Chester Cathedral", "seems to have run the whole length of the east cloister above the Parlour, the Slype (passage), and Vestibule of the Chapter House and, in later times, at least, over the cloister itself."

49. A number of buildings in the Rows at the centre of Chester are constructed over mediaeval stone undercrofts or crypts. Their original purpose is uncertain, but they were probably used as workshops or for storage. The Roman hypocaust, discovered in the early eighteenth century, can be seen in the basement of 39, Bridge Street.

50. Lleweni Hall was the home of Robert Cotton, Sir Lynch's son and Mrs. Thrale's cousin. Robert and Frances Cotton entertained the party here for three weeks, arranging visits to friends and excursions to places of interest in the neighbourhood. Pennant describes the Hall thus: "Lleweni, notwithstanding it lies on a flat, has most pleasing views of the mountains on each side of the vale;

the town and Castle of Denbigh form most capital objects, at the distance of two miles." It was once one of the greatest houses in North Wales, seat of the powerful Salusbury family who had settled in the area before the time of Henry III. The interior contained a fine Gothic hall, fitted up as an armoury, and a drawing-room hung with Gobelin tapestries. The Hall was sold in 1781 and, after mixed fortunes, was pulled down in 1817. All that remains today is the ground floor of the two-storey gateway to the Hall, with its entrance arch and windows bricked up. Built at right angles to this is a large house, circa 1750, believed to be the Dower House, now a farmhouse. A short distance away stands a vast, ruinous coach-house cum stabling block.

51. Bachygraig had been in Mrs. Thrale's family for generations. The house was built by the eminent merchant, Sir Richard Clough (1530?-70) in 1567-9; his initials are still over the walled-up arch of the gateway and the date 1567 is carved over a door nearby. Clough was an eminent merchant who acted as a factor in Antwerp for Sir Thomas Gresham [See Johnson Note 60]. In 1567 he married Katherine of Berain; they had two daughters from whom Hester Lynch Salusbury (Mrs. Thrale) was descended. He was buried in Whitchurch. Pennant described the house thus: "It consistsof a mansion, and three sides, enclosing a square court. The first consists of a vast hall, and parlour: the rest of it rises into six wonderful stories, including the cupola, and forms from the second floor the figure of a pyramid: the rooms are small, and inconvenient. The bricks are admirable and appear to have been made in Holland or by Dutchmen on the spot. [They were made locally. Ed.] ... the model of the house was probably brought from Flanders where this species of building is not unfrequent." In due course, the Bachygraig estate came into the possession of the Salusbury family and Mrs. Thrale's father, John, was born there in 1707. However, because of debts brought about by his own fecklessness, he was unable to live there and moved out to Bodfel Hall near Pwllheli. Thus the house gradually fell into the decayed state in which Mrs. Thrale saw it. She found it very dirty, particularly the stairs, and she required some persuasion to go up, but Johnson prevailed upon her. "My mistress" was his favourite epithet for her; he also frequently referred to Mr. Thrale as "my master", indicating at once their relationship and his dependence. By 1817 the main wing of the house was demolished, the cupola and weathervane being moved by Mr. Piozzi to Brynbella up the road where they still adorn the coach-house. Today two wings of the original building survive, though much altered. The gatehouse wing is used as the farmhouse. The arch has been bricked up, the windows altered, and the tower has been moved from over

the arch to the corner of the house. In the other wing, the loggia has been bricked up although the pillars are visible. The house stands in a sheltered position under the hill and there is still woodland to the rear and sides. The 16th c. warehouses, which Clough built with a view to developing trade in the area, are now used as barns and the main one is impressive. The estate was sold to the Roberts family in the mid-19th c. and has been farmed by them ever since. The present owner, Mr. D. C. Roberts, and his wife also offer bed and breakfast.

52. The fifteenth century oak stalls with their fine canopy work, which Johnson saw in the chancel, were cleaned and restored in 1870.

canonicus: a canon.

prebend: a canon who holds a prebend, i.e. a stipend derived from cathedral revenues.

cancellarius: chancellor, in charge of the cathedral schools.

thesaurarius: treasurer, in charge of the fabric.

praecentor: precentor, in charge of music.

The refurbished Translators' Chapel principally commemorates the work of William Morgan, Bishop from 1601-04, who translated the Bible into Welsh while Vicar of Llanrhaiadr-ym-Mochnant [See Johnson Note 112].

The restored Lady Chapel has some attractive modern furniture.

53. Dr. Jonathan Shipley. He lived in the Bishop's Palace, now known as The Old Palace, which is situated towards the bottom of the hill near the river. The Old Palace, a not un-imposing stone house, has been converted into flats. The words "and design a room" suggest the Bishop planned to house his collection in a special room.

54. William Lloyd (1627-1717), Bishop of St. Asaph, came from a family of bishops and clerics. At one time he had been an Army Chaplain. [See Johnson's entry for August 8] He was an uncompromising Anglican and a prominent supporter of the Glorious Revolution of 1688. In that year he had gone to the Tower for refusing to permit the publication of James II's declaration for liberty of conscience. He died Bishop of Worcester in 1717. His friend Henry Dodwell, a non-juror, visited him at St. Asaph.

55. Denbigh Castle was built by Henry de Lacy, Earl of Lincoln, between 1282 and 1311. It was planned round a large courtyard enclosing the highest point of the hilltop. It endured a six months siege in the Civil War before surrendering to the Parliamentarians in 1646. The façade of the impressive Gatehouse, with its

arch and niche, which formerly held a statue of Henry de Lacy, is at present being restored.

56. St. Hilary's Chapel, built c. 1300, continued to be used as the parish church because the new 16th c. parish church (Whitchurch) was built on an ancient site over a mile from the town. The Chapel was unroofed in 1904 and only the tower now remains.

57. Robert Dudley, Earl of Leicester, started to build this church in 1579 with the apparent intention of transferring the cathedral from St. Asaph to Denbigh. It was never completed, partly because of the "public hatred he had incurred by his tyranny" and partly because the Earl of Essex later borrowed (and never repaid) the money that had been collected for its completion. When Johnson visited it, it had been converted into a barn, but the wall of the north aisle and the east end remain as Johnson saw them.

58. The Chapel of Lleweni was part of the Carmelite Friary on the outskirts of Denbigh. It was founded towards the end of the 13th c. by Sir John Salusbury of Lleweni who was buried in the Friary Church. It was destroyed by fire in 1898 and is now simply a shell near the traffic lights at the bottom of the hill leading up to the town centre.

59. Whitchurch (Eglwys Wen) is now known as St. Marcella's (Llanfarchell) and is both the mother and the parish church of Denbigh. A Perpendicular church with twin naves, it was neglected for long periods but it has recently completed its third restoration, and, although plain without, is most attractive within. It contains the fine, painted alabaster table-tomb of Sir John Salusbury (d. 1578) and his wife.

60. Humphrey Lloyd (1527-68) was an Oxford-educated physician in Denbigh and M.P. for the town, but he was better known as an antiquary and author of several significant works. He was a friend of Sir Richard Clough [See Note 51] who introduced him to the scholar, geographer and publisher, Abraham Ortelius of Amsterdam. As a result he prepared the manuscript of a map of Wales and a map of England and Wales which were published by Ortelius in 1573. The map of Wales continued to be re-printed until 1741.

His monument has been cleaned but most of the inscription below it is illegible.

Notes on Johnson's Diary 69

61. William Camden (1551-1623), antiquary and historian, author of "Britannia".

62. When Mrs. Piozzi read Johnson's remark about the old clerk only receiving a crown from her, she commented, "The poor clerk had probably never seen a crown in his possession before. Things were very different A.D. 1774, from what they are today."

63. Llannerch was originally famous for its superb late 17th c. formal gardens built on terraces descending steeply to the river below. It was created by Mutton Davies after he returned from the Grand Tour in 1658 having been mightily impressed by Italianate gardens. The gardens, complete with walled enclosures, were destroyed in Victorian times; at the same time the house lost its pitched roof and was re-modelled into its present form. It is now converted into flats. The estate has been broken up; the lodge (extended) is a Residential Home for the Elderly and nearby is a golf driving range. But one can still get some idea of the former splendour of the gardens from the existing terraces.

The owner, John Davies was the great grandson of the Welsh antiquary, Robert Davies, who formed a collection of Welsh MSS. Robert Davies died in 1728 and

The terrace at Llannerch.

there is a fine statue of him in Roman dress by Sir Henry Cheere in Mold Church.

64. Mrs. Thrale later wrote that, "Johnson said that I flattered the people to whose houses we went. I was saucy, and said I was obliged to be civil for two - meaning himself and me. He replied, nobody would thank me for compliments they did not understand. At Gwaynynog (Mr. Myddleton's), however, he was flattered, and was happy of course."

65. The fascinating complex of buildings at St. Winefride's Well has not changed in essentials since Dr. Johnson and Mrs. Thrale visited it. For centuries the well has been a major Roman Catholic shrine and place of pilgrimage and it continues to attract many pilgrims and visitors.

Legend has it that Winefride, fleeing to the church built by her uncle, St. Beuno, to escape the transparent intentions of a chieftain called Caradoc, was caught by him and beheaded. St. Beuno appeared, placed her head back on her shoulders and restored her to life, while Caradoc sank into the ground and disappeared. Where Winefride's head fell, a spring gushed forth with healing powers.

A two-storied chapel over the well was built at the end of the fifteenth century. The lower chapel encloses the spring and its basin and it is here that pilgrims go down the steps into the pool, traditionally passing through the water three times. The spring also feeds an outside bath, though the water looks rather uninviting. The shrine is open for bathers winter and summer; men 8 - 9 a.m., women 9 - 10 a.m. The well-chapel was damaged and St. Winefride's statue destroyed in 1637. The present statue, which has a line round the neck to indicate where the head was severed, was installed in 1888.

The charming upper chapel looks rather different from when Dr. Johnson saw it, because in 1723 the Protestants converted it into a schoolroom and gave it a false, sloping roof. However, the chapel was recently restored by the Department of the Environment and is now open to the public.

There was much concern at the shrine in 1917 when mining operations at Halkyn diverted the stream and the well ran dry. Luckily, another spring was found, though considerably less powerful, and diverted to it.

66. This is the Parish Church of Holywell; it was rebuilt (except for the tower) in 1770 and remodelled in 1885. Because of its position under the hill, the bells could not be heard in the town so a man went round with a bell fixed to his leg. Bell and knee-pad are kept in the church.

67. The Greenfield Valley below Holywell was the cradle of the Industrial Revolution in Wales. The force of the stream from St. Winefride's Well provided power for a variety of industries (forges, wire mills, lead mining, copper and brass battery mills) stretching for a mile and a half down the valley to the banks of the Dee Estuary. These industries were rapidly developing at the time of Johnson's visit. The first copper works was built by Thomas Patten's Warrington Company about 1755. Copper ingots, made from copper ore mined at Parys Mountain in Anglesey and smelted at the Stanley Works near St. Helens, were brought from Liverpool to the Greenfield wharf on the Dee. In 1766 Patten erected the Battery Works, so called because pots and pans were shaped there from sheets of brass held under heavy tilt hammers. The lapis caluminaris Johnson noticed is the calamine lead ore from which zinc is extracted for use in the manufacture of brass. A few years later in 1777 came the cotton industry and an important expansion of the copper industry into the manufacture of copper sheathing and bolts for the wooden hulls of merchantmen and men o' war. The area had one of the fastest population growth rates in Great Britain between 1750 and 1800. Remains of the various mills and workings can still be seen in the valley which has been creditably developed as a Heritage Park.

68. Rhuddlan Castle, constructed 1277-82, was one of the six castles built by Edward I to subdue North Wales – the others are Flint, Conwy, Beaumaris, Caernarfon, and Harlech. During the Civil War the castle surrendered to the Parliamentary forces in 1646 and two years later it was made untenable. Time and decay, aided by its being an easy source for building materials, have reduced it to its present state.

69. The cascade at Dyserth is still an attractive and impressive waterfall. Pennant wrote of it: "The stream, which is little inferior to that of Holywell, flows principally from a single well, called Fynnon Asaph or St. Asaph's well, in a dingle in the parish of Cwm about a mile distant. The fountain is inclosed with stone in a polygonal form, and had formerly its Votaries like that of St. Winefride." I could not find the well. Mrs. Piozzi recalls: "He teased Mrs. Cotton about her dry cascade till she was ready to cry: the waterfall being near her maiden residence made her, I suppose, partial to the place; for she sent us thither to be entertained, and expected much praise at our return." Earlier, in November 1772, Johnson had written to Mrs. Thrale after visiting Chatsworth ... "when one has seen the Ocean, cascades are but little things."

70. This was almost certainly Pengwern, the seat of Edward Lloyd (c. 1710-95),

who was High Sheriff of Flintshire in 1768/69 and created a baronet in 1778. Pengwern Hall is today one of the Royal Society's Schools for the education and training of Mentally Handicapped Children and Adults (RSMHCA).

71. Flatus (L) = wind. Ipecacuanha (an emetic made from a South American plant), wine of antimony, and tartar emetic were all standard drugs used to cause vomiting.

72. Their amiable, fifty year old host, John Myddleton, had been Mayor of Denbigh and he made an excellent impression on Johnson. He had a fine library and Horace Walpole used to send him books printed at Strawberry Hill. He was also a close friend and correspondent of Thomas Pennant (1726-98), the celebrated naturalist and traveller. There is an interesting sidelight on his hospitality in a letter from Richard Twining to his brother in 1785:
"We breakfasted at Colonel Myddleton's at Gwynanog. It is not so highly ornamented as Mr. Yorke's at Erdigg, but it is much more wild and picturesque, and contains a much greater variety of scene... . I could not help saying to Hughes, 'I wish I could show my brother this spot.' Colonel Myddleton immediately turned round; 'Bring him next summer; I have plenty of beds and shall be heartily glad to see you both.' "

Mr Myddleton invited Johnson and his friends to visit him on their return from the Lleyn peninsula and they stayed at Gwaynynog from 29th August to 6th September.

73. Evan Evans (Ieuan Fardd) 1731-89, was a scholar, poet and cleric, who collected early Welsh poetry and translated it into English. He established his reputation in 1764 with *Some Specimens of the Poetry of the Ancient Welsh Bards.* He was undoubtedly the greatest Welsh scholar of his age and prominently involved in the literary and antiquarian renaissance in Wales in the 18th c. He felt the primary need of Welsh scholarship was the publication of the texts of the principal manuscripts dealing with the history and the literature of Wales. He tried hard, but without success, to raise funds for this project. His heavy drinking put off potential sponsors and was also a factor in his failure to gain advancement in the Church. He died in poverty and disillusionment.

74. Rev. William Worthington, D.D. (1703-78), Vicar of Llanrhaiadr-ym-Mochnant was a friend of Johnson and wrote many books on religious subjects. Johnson received an invitation from him while at Caernarfon and the party stayed at his house on 8th September on their return journey.

75. Siôn Dafydd Rhys (1534-1609) is a typical example of the Renaissance Welshman. After travelling extensively on the Continent and becoming a physician, he eventually returned to Wales to practise. In 1592 he published his famous Welsh Grammar. Written in Latin, this consisted of a grammar of the Welsh language plus a tedious discussion of Welsh prosody. His aim was to make known outside Wales the peculiarities of the Welsh language and the main features of the Bardic tradition. Sadly, the work is of slight merit and one is surprised that Johnson should think it worth being re-published.

76. This refers to the last act of Beaumont and Fletcher's *The Maid's Tragedy*, originally revised by Edmund Waller and further amended by Francis Atterbury.

77. Johnson was right about the tower but the church is no longer mean. The interesting carved oak pulpit came from Lleweni when the house was demolished.

78. Phocylites was a 6th c. B.C. poet from Miletus whose couplets and hexameters, a few of which survive, embody moral observations and precepts.

79. John Leland (1506?-52) was the earliest of our modern antiquaries. He travelled throughout England in 1534-43 but his grand design resulted, in effect, in a compilation of ill-digested notes. In his "Itinerary" the Lichfield School entry refers to an institution set up by Henry VII which included a "Hospital" and "a Schoole-Mr. to teach Grammer that hath 10 l [pounds] by the yeare, and an Under-Schoole-Mr. that hath 5 l by the yeare."

80. Sir Edward Lloyd actually owned Maesmynnan in 1774. His brothers and sisters lived in various houses belonging to him. The house, now a private nursing home, is near Bodfari on the road to Mold. Mrs. Thrale's comment on the house is accurate. The rather unimposing exterior has recently been pebble-dashed. I could find no trace of the walled garden, but the grounds must obviously have been attractive in the past.

81. "A Journey to Mequinez, the Residence of the present Emperor of Fez and Morocco, on the Occasion of Commodore Stewart's Embassy thither, for the Redemption of the British Captives, in the Year 1721."

82. The Reverend Joseph Wasse's Greek verses to Richard Bentley, the great classicist, appeared in the sixth number of Jebb's "Bibliotheca Literaria" in 1723. This learned periodical, much of it written in Latin, found little favour and closed after ten issues.

83. Little meat; i.e. Johnson dined modestly. A motion achieved without taking a purge.

84. References to Johnson's reading at Lleweni. The "Letter to Caesarius", formerly attributed to Chrysostom, appeared in the fourth number of the "Bibliotheca Literaria". Erasmus's letter: "Sacris Virginibus".

85. A weakness of the knees, not without some pain in walking, which I feel increased after I have dined.

86. Levet was a dour, silent Yorkshireman, "obscurely wise, and coarsely kind", who emerged from a bizarre background to become an intimate friend of Johnson and to live in his house for many years. He had acquired a smattering of medical knowledge in Paris and on his return to England he earned, in Wain's words, "a meagre living by mixing ointment and powders for the ailments of coachmen, fishporters and bricklayers."

87. The popular Conwy Races were held annually on the Morfa Conwy, a stretch of flat land forming a promontory at the mouth of the river now largely occupied by the local golf club. A King's Plate was granted to be run for and this race continued until 1794. No trace of the racecourse remains; this tract of land has now been bisected by the new North Wales Coast Road.

88. Johnson was fortunate. The original cliff road, which was more of a narrow zig-zag path, was notoriously unsafe. In *Patterson's Roads* of 1822, Penmaenmawr inspires the editor to a hectic passage of Romantic bravura, thus: "Penmaenmawr is an immense rock that protrudes itself into the sea, and rises above its level to the height of 1540 feet; the pass over it was formerly both rugged and dangerous, and could scarcely fail to impress the traveller with emotions of fear, naturally arising from the impending precipice hanging over his head, and momentarily threatening by its shivering aspect to overwhelm or hurry him down headlong into the dreadful abyss a hundred fathoms below, where the roaring ocean foamed against the perpendicular base of the mountain on which he stood.

In the year 1772 application was however made to Parliament, and liberal assistance granted for improving and securing this part of the road to Holyhead... and under the judicious superintendence of Mr. John Sylvester, a civil engineer, a road has been made that will hereafter perhaps be considered as one of the most sublime terraces in the British Isles. This road winds round the mountain, and is now protected towards the sea by a strong wall about 5' high, which is supported in many places by deep walls below; but even yet, to a timid traveller a scene of horror is presented by the amazingly abrupt precipices of rock, variegated with fragments and ruins, that appear ready to fall, and crush the traveller to atoms."

Today the summit of Penmaenmawr appears quite different. The headland and the adjoining hillsides have been extensively quarried and disfigured for generations for their quartz dolerite which is one of the best road-making stones.

89. Baron Hill was situated in a splendid position on a hillside above Beaumaris; the view from it was the boast of Anglesey. Its famous grounds, laid out by the well-known garden designer, William Emes, "received all the embellishments that art could accomplish, with a number of ornamental buildings judiciously placed in corresponding situations." The house was built in 1618 by Sir Richard Bulkeley but much altered by Samuel Wyatt several years after Johnson's visit. It was burnt down in the early nineteenth century and a new house was erected on the site in 1830-35. The shell of this building stands today in the park. When Johnson and Mrs. Thrale were there, the owner was Thomas James, seventh Viscount Bulkeley, Constable of the Castle of Beaumaris and Chamberlain of North Wales. The Bulkeleys were the most prominent landowners in Anglesey for generations.

90. Beaumaris Castle was built between 1295-1330 but never completed. It was perhaps the high point of mediaeval military architecture, with its geometric plan emphasising the concept of concentric defence. Like the other Edwardian castles in North Wales, it was built by the sea so that the garrison could be supplied and reinforced by water. Johnson and Mrs. Thrale were rightly impressed by the immense strength of the fortress and by the moat which was at least 50' wide. No-one has so far discovered the well.

91. The Reverend William Lloyd had only recently been appointed headmaster of Beaumaris Grammar School, which was built close to the moat of the castle. Today all that is left is the headmaster's house and a small section of the school which were converted into a small Community Centre in 1971. Over the porch of the house is inscribed 1603 DH – this refers to David Hughes, a local benefactor who built the school.

92. Thomas Roberts (c. 1698-1778) was Notary Public and Registrar of the Diocese of Bangor from 1754 till 1778. It was a reponsible post because the

proving of wills and other legal business passed through the Diocesan Registry.

93. Caernarfon Castle (1283-1327), strategically situated at the southern end of the Menai Strait, was built as a fortress-palace by Edward I for the English Princes of Wales. It remained the capital of the Principality until 1536. The castle was built on a peninsula virtually surrounded by water – the Strait, the River Saint or Seiont, and the Cadnant brook, the latter now covered over.

The ivy Mrs. Thrale noticed here and at other castles is confirmed by contemporary and later prints but, as in the case of the other Edwardian castles, it was removed when Caernarfon was repaired and restored. Johnson could not find the well but the entrance to it was probably hidden by the rubble and rubbish he remarked upon. The remains of some lead pipes he noticed were those which led water from a lead-lined cistern down through the walls to the adjoining kitchens. There had originally been a great ditch on the north side of the castle but this had been filled and obscured by the time of Johnson's visit, and the moat was not dug out until late in the nineteenth century. Lt. Troughton [See Johnson Note 96 and Mrs. Thrale's entry for 20th August] was right to be cynical about claims that the son of Edward I and Queen Eleanor was born in a small room in the Eagle Tower – very much an old guide's tale. The prince was certainly born within the castle walls in 1284, but this happened in the early timbered apartments swept away by later building. The party are to be congratulated on climbing up the Eagle Tower. If they went right to the top of one of the turrets, then Johnson's figure of 169 steps is pretty accurate.

94. General Pasquale de Paoli, the Corsican patriot, had sought refuge in England in 1769 and Johnson had met him in October of that year. He commented that General Paoli had the loftiest port of any man he had ever seen. Paoli eventually became a member of the Johnson circle and a frequent visitor to Streatham.

95. At this time Sir Thomas Wynn was Lord Lieutenant of Caernarfonshire and MP for the County. He was created Lord Newborough in 1776.

96. Lieut. Ellis Troughton, R.N. Aged forty four, he was on half-pay when he encountered Johnson.

97. Johnson and Mrs. Thrale worshipped at St. Mary's Church, also known as the Garrison Chapel, where the service was conducted in English. This unusual chapel was built in the north-west corner of the walled town in 1307. The base

of the corner tower was converted into a commodious vestry. The Parish church referred to is the ancient church of Llanbeblig, the mother-church of Caernarfon, built near the Roman fort of Segontium on the road to Beddgelert.

98. The former Lady Catherine Perceval, daughter of the second Earl of Egmont.

99. Bridget, wife of Colonel Glynn Wynn who was Sir Thomas's brother and MP for Caernarfon Boroughs, 1768-90.

100. Impropriation: tithes or ecclesiastical property placed in lay hands. Even in her father's time, Bridge had trouble here setting and collecting the tithes which were based on an estimate of the parishoners' corn crops.

101. Mona was the Roman name for Anglesey.

102. Clynnog Fawr is a splendid perpendicular church with a large east window overlooking the road. It is the traditional burial place of St. Beuno [see Johnson Note 65] and was an important shrine for pilgrims on their way to Bardsey Island.

103. John Griffith (1742-94), the owner of Cefnamwlch, inherited the estate in

The Parish Church of St. Beuno, Clynnog Fawr.

1752. As a young lieutenant he fought at the battle of Minden in 1759; he died unmarried. He was the son of 'Madam Sidney Griffith' (d. 1752), a notable, if somewhat bizarre, figure in Methodist circles. Distancing herself from her drunken boor of a husband, she met, influenced and became involved with Howel Harris [See Thrale Note 57]. Harris, an enthusiastic evangelist, was one of the founding fathers of Methodism in the religious revival in Wales and he was considered the greatest spiritual force of his generation. "Madam Griffith' laid claim to prophetic powers and Harris, despite protests, took her advice unquestioningly and she accompanied him everywhere. The scandal, real or imagined, led to a breach between Harris and other Methodist leaders. "Madam Griffith' was unable to heal it and she died shortly afterwards.

104. This is Dolbadarn Castle, much celebrated by artists. Built by Llewellyn the Great circa 1170, it commanded the Llanberis Pass, the route between Caernarfon and Anglesey and the Conwy Valley. It was partly dismantled after the English Conquest. All that remains today is the circular keep with its external spiral staircase and the foundations of the curtain wall and other buildings. It is still a stiff scramble for the middle-aged. Because of the impact on the landscape of the enormous Dinorwic slate quarries, the view from the keep is much changed since Johnson's visit.

105. Mr. Thrale was short-sighted and could not see the goats browsing on Snowdon, but he promised Queeny a penny for every goat she could show him. Dr. Johnson, who enjoyed computation, kept the score.

106. The castle and walled town of Conwy was built between 1283 and 1289 on a promontory formed by the river Gyffin and the river Conwy. Johnson appears to have had a particular interest in wells and water-supply – and rightly so, for a castle without an independent water supply would soon be forced to surrender.

107. This attractive house is largely unchanged today and has been in the Burton family for over a hundred years. There is some evidence to suggest that during his stay Johnson was concerned in the design of the two principal rooms on the south front. Certainly Johnson was happy and amused here and Myddleton was equally flattered by the visit. To mark it, he later erected an urn on the bank of the tiny River Ystrad where Johnson delighted to stand and recite poetry. The tall Grecian urn stands on a square pedestal with this inscription:

> This spot was often dignified by the presence of
> SAMUEL JOHNSON, L.L.D.
> whose Moral Writings, exactly conformable to the
> Precepts of Christianity,
> gave Ardour to Virtue, and Confidence to Truth.

It appears from a letter Johnson wrote to Mrs. Thrale in 1777 that he had got wind of Myddleton's idea which was little to his taste. "Mr Myddleton's erection of an urn", he wrote, "looks like an intention to bury me alive; I would as willingly see my friend, however benevolent and hospitable, quietly inurned. Let him think, for the present, of some more acceptable memorial." The urn, which stands in a beautiful spot at the foot of a steep slope, was restored in 1975 but has since suffered some frost damage.

The so-called 'Johnson's Cottage' (he never actually stayed in it) is a short distance away downstream among woodland. When Johnson visited the cottage he would have seen the following inscription or motto over the door, put up by Mr Myddleton in 1768:

> Around this homely Cot, this humble shed
> If Health if Competence, and Virtue tread;
> Though no proud Column grace the gaudy Door,
> Where sculptur'd Elegance parades it O'er,
> Nor Pomp without, nor Pageantry within,
> Nor splendid show, nor Ornament is seen;
> The swain shall look with Pity on the Great,
> Nor barter Quiet for a King's Estate.

The cottage is now an utter ruin, the present owners (Mr. and Mrs. T. Smith) having been forced several years ago to remove the roof for safety reasons. But they rescued the inscription and this is now at Gwaynynog. Also at the house is an ancient, twisted walking stick reputed to have been used by Johnson during his stay there.

Mrs. Piozzi relates: "Dr. Johnson... . asked of one of our sharp currents in North Wales – Has this Brook e'er a name? – and received for answer – Why, dear Sir, this is the River Ustrad - Let us, said he, turning to his friend, jump over it directly, and shew them how an *Englishman* should treat a *Welsh* River."

108. This was the Rev. Robert Myddleton, rector of Denbigh 1772-97, the younger brother of their host.

109. The beautifully-kept Parish Church of St. Giles, built in the late 15th and early 16th centuries.

In the churchyard is the tomb of Elihu Yale, founder of Yale University in Newhaven, Connecticut.

110. The owner at this time was Richard Myddleton, MP for Denbigh Boroughs and Lord Lieutenant of Denbighshire. It seems probable that the party stayed the night at the Castle although the owner was away.

111. Many years later, Mrs. Piozzi related that it was probably on the 7th of September that, on their way from Wrexham to Chirk, they passed through Ruabon where the following occurrence took place: "A Welsh parson of mean abilities, though a good heart, struck with reverence at the sight of Dr. Johnson, whom he had heard of as the greatest man living, could not find any words to answer his inquiries concerning a motto round somebody's arms which adorned a tombstone in Ruabon churchyard. If I remember right the words were:'Heb Dw, Heb Dym, Dw o' diggon.' [This is the motto of the Myddleton family: 'Without God – without all! God is all-sufficient.' There is no trace now of the tombstone in the churchyard.] And though of no very difficult construction, the gentleman seemed wholly confounded and unable to explain them, till Mr. Johnson, having picked out the meaning little by little, said to the man, 'Heb is a preposition, I believe, sir, is it not?' My countryman, recovering some spirits upon the sudden question, cried out, 'So I humbly presume, sir,' very comically."

112. Dr. Worthington, former Prebendary of York, died on 6th October 1778 aged seventy-five. Johnson thus notices his death in a letter to Mrs. Thrale: "My clerical friend Worthington is dead. I have known him long – and to die is dreadful. I believe he was a very good man."

The Old Vicarage is little changed structurally from the time when Johnson and his party stayed there. However, it is now in private hands and has been metamorphosed into "Llys Morgan", a guest house offering B. & B. It was in this house that the Bible was first translated into Welsh by the Rev. William Morgan (1545-1604), who was Vicar of Llanrhaiadr from 1578 to 1595 and later became Bishop of St. Asaph. [See Johnson Note 52] The translation was published in 1588. He was assisted by Edmwnd Prys (1544-1623), Archdeacon of Merioneth, whose metrical version of the Psalms was published as an appendix to the 1621 edition of the Welsh Book of Common Prayer.

113. This was a famous pony fair.

114. This is because St. Oswald's Church was originally a conventual

foundation, not simply a parish church.

115. This is the famous Pistyll Rhaeadr, some four miles north west of Llanrhaiadr. Approached by a narrow winding road from the village, it is a stunning prospect with sheer cliffs and tree-clad rocky cliffs on either side. It is the highest waterfall in Wales with a fall of 240 feet, broken by a rock arch two thirds of the way down. There is a very steep path to the top of the cliffs from which the waterfall may be reached. It is fed by a stream, the Afon Disgynfa, which, rising a couple of miles away in the Berwyn hills, tumbles down to the edge of the cliff in a series of attractive waterfalls. There is no sign here of any "reservoir made to supply it" – unless Johnson meant the area around the stream acting as a natural collecting point for water. The room for entertainment has blossomed into a full-blown, stone-built cafe with a portico of rough-hewn tree-trunks, plus a car park and toilets. The reference to Thomas, the second Lord Lyttleton, is puzzling. Mrs. Thrale does not mention him and the party did not visit Hagley Hall until a week later.

116. John Gwynn, architect and native of Shrewsbury, was at this time completing the English Bridge across the Severn.

117. Dr. John Taylor (1704-66) was a Cambridge classicist who left part of his large and valuable collection of books to Shrewsbury School where he was educated. The school moved to new premises in 1882; the original building served for some years as an art gallery and then after renovation reopened several years ago as the Castle Gates Public Library.

118. The Quarry is now an attractive public park in the bend of the Severn. Above it rises the cupola and golden cross of the splendid late 18th c. Greek-revival church of St. Chad's, with its circular nave and graceful columns and gallery. On the ridge across the river stand the buildings of Shrewsbury School.

119. This was Old St. Chad's, a great cruciform church built in the first half of the 13th c. It was largely destroyed when its massive central tower collapsed in 1788. The remains, the shell of the Lady Chapel, can be seen in the angle between Belmont and Princess Street.

120. Dr. Adams, later Master of Pembroke College, Oxford, was Rector of St. Chad's and a friend of Johnson. He lived in an early 17th c. house, known as Rowley's Mansion, in Hill's Lane. William Rowley, of Worfield near Bridgnorth, originally established himself as a draper and brewer in a large

timber-framed late 16th c. house. This has been extensively restored and is now a museum, known as Rowley's House Museum. In 1618, having prospered considerably, he built the first brick house in the town onto the Elizabethan structure and this as known as Rowley's Mansion. It is now an integral part of the museum and, although extensively gutted, the great ceiling beams remain as does the plaster ceiling on the ground floor. The exterior of the Mansion contrasts unfavourably with the restored Rowley's House but no doubt this will be attended to in due course.

121. The Norman tower, some seventy feet high and far from perpendicular, is the only surviving part of the castle.

122. Edwin Sandys, second Baron Sandys, succeeded his father in 1770. In 1769 he married Anna Maria, widow of William Paine King, who brought him an enormous fortune. Lord Sandys, who was young Ralph Thrale's godfather, and his wife were frequent visitors at Streatham. Mrs. Piozzi recalled that Johnson said "that he had never had quite as much as he wished of wall-fruit except once in his life, and that was when we were all together at Ombersley." Ombersley Court is still the family seat.

123. The compiler of this chronicle, *Liber Cronicarum*, printed in 1493, was Hartman Schedel, a physician of Nuremburg. It is still in the cathedral library.

124. Little Hagley (now demolished) was the home of Mr. W. H. Lyttelton, later Lord Westcote, a friend and contemporary of Thrale's, with whom he had made the Grand Tour. He was the other godfather of young Ralph Thrale. The visit, however, was not a success and contrasted disagreeably with the party's reception at Ombersley. Lyttleton, who had been a widower for nearly ten years, had recently remarried and he and his wife (formerly Caroline Bristow) proved unexpectedly poor hosts.

125. This was Hagley Hall owned by their host's nephew, Thomas, Lord Lyttelton, generally known to the family as 'Naughty Tom'. He was not at home. The old Hall had been rebuilt as a Palladian mansion between 1756 and 1760 by the 1st Lord Lyttelton and it much impressed the visitors, both Mr. and Mrs. Thrale noting with approval that the kitchen and domestic areas were nowhere in evidence.

The park was laid out from the mid-1740s and, in terms of garden design, was one of the most influential landscape gardens of the mid-18th c. The formal

Italianate and French gardens which had dominated European garden design were now being supplanted in England by a more natural and 'picturesque' landscape under the influence of William Kent and 'Capability' Brown. This change to gardening as landscape painting was echoed and encouraged by the literature of the period (Addison, Pope, Thomason, Shenstone) and particularly by the writings and paintings of William Gilpin (1724-1804). He defined those features which constitute the picturesque and he exercised a profound influence on the development of Picturesque taste during the second half of the 18th c.

The garden at Hagley was much admired by Walpole who wrote: "You might draw but I cannot describe the enchanting beauties of Hagley Park." It was designed to stimulate certain ideas to which gardening, painting and poetry each contributed. James Thomson (1700-48), though no gardener, enlarged and revised his poem, *The Seasons*, at his patron's home at Hagley, finding inspiration in his musings and meditations among natural scenery.

Today Hagley Hall is still the home of the Lytteltons – the cricketing Cobhams – and retains its splendid prospects, especially to the west. It contains what is considered the finest Rococo plasterwork in England, created by Francesco Vassalli. In the library hangs a portrait by Reynolds of Johnson's host at Little Hagley (W. H. Lyttelton) painted for the Thrale's house at Streatham. There is a good view of the Hall and estate from a track beyond the church that leads uphill for half a mile to "Milton's Seat", a bench in a clearing on the hillside inscribed with lines from Book V of *Paradise Lost*.

126. These are to the west end of the Church of St. John the Baptist, the parish church of Hagley. Among them is a fine monument by Roubiliac to Lucy, first wife of the 1st Lord Lyttelton. It consists of an urn, decorated with a garland, a female figure and the name Luciae. Beside the urn is a naked child and an extinguished torch – all symbols of mortality [See Mrs Thrale's entry for 18th September].

127. John, second Viscount Dudley, who had succeeded to the title in May.

128. Sir Edward Lyttleton succeeded his uncle in 1742. He owned Pillaton Hall and Teddersley Hay in Staffordshire.

129. The Leasowes, near Halesowen, was the home of the poet William Shenstone (1714-63), who had been a contemporary of Johnson's at Pembroke. Johnson damned him with faint praise in his *Life of Shenstone*. Shenstone devoted most of his life to the development and embellishment of his estate.

Johnson concludes: "He spent his estate in adorning it, and his death was probably hastened by his anxieties. He was a lamp that spent its oil in blazing. It is said that if he had lived a little longer, he would have been assisted by a pension." It appears that Lord Loughborough applied to Lord Bute to procure Shenstone a pension but it is uncertain if the King was approached. Shenstone's death resolved the issue.Although the Leasowes had only a brief life – some thirty years – it was, like neighbouring Hagley Hall, one of the most influential lanscape gardens of the period and attracted many visitors, including Lyttelton and Thomson. Shenstone developed streams in a narrow cleft on his estate to make a series of cascades descending into a lake and this, with a circuit walk, formed what he called his "Arcadian farm". Shenstone, like Thomson, strove to express his poetic imaginings in terms of the external world and found his vehicle in the landscape garden. His garden thus became "a perfect picture of his mind" and echoed his poetic fancies.

Mrs. Piozzi recalls Johnson remarking about gardens that, "that water was most to be prized which contained much fish". When he learned that Shenstone did not care if there were any fish in the streams and lake he was so fond of, he erupted: "as if one could fill one's belly with hearing soft murmurs, or looking at rough cascades."

Today the Leasowes is a popular public park bisecting the Halesowen Golf Club. Much of Shenstone's creation – the woodland, the bridge and the remains of the cascades – can still be enjoyed. The perimeter walk can still be traced and the lake, where Mrs. Thrale sat by the boathouse (now gone) and composed verses, is the haunt of local anglers. It is encouraging to report that the local authority has embarked upon a restoration programme for the garden.

130. Edmund Hector was a school-friend of Johnson's and practised as a surgeon in Birmingham. His house at No. 1, Old Square, later formed part of the Stork Hotel but was demolished in 1882 when Corporation Street was made. In the transformed town centre, Old Square is now a shopping area below street level.

131. This was the factory of Clay and Gibbons. Clay, like many of his contemporaries, found japanning very popular. In 1772 he abandoned the paper pulp process in favour of pressing sheets of paper closely together, and took out a patent for his invention. His business premises were in New Hall Street. After showing his goods to Queen Charlotte in 1793 he styled himself "Japanner in Ordinary to Her Majesty".

132. Rotten-stone is a silica-based powder mainly used for polishing metals. Tea-board = tea tray.

133. Matthew Boulton was one of the great engineers of the 18th c. A year after this visit James Watt went into partnership with him at the Soho works in Birmingham to build steam-engines, and the next twenty-five years saw a remarkable period of invention and engineering development. When Boulton showed Boswell round the works in 1776, he exalted, "I sell here, Sir, what all the world desires to have – POWER."

134. Blenheim Palace, designed by Vanbrugh in the Italian Renaissance style, was presented to John Churchill, Duke of Marlborough, by a grateful nation for his services in the French Wars. It stands in the former royal estate of Woodstock, which was granted to him at the same time. The park, some 2,700 acres in area, was the greatest achievement of Capability Brown. Brown (1715-83) had worked with William Kent at Stowe and together they effected a revolution in garden design, one that exerted immense influence on the development of the 18th c. garden as 'landscape painting'. Brown went on to work on more than 150 estates and gardens. The paintings and the contents of the Library were largely dispersed by auction between 1875 and 1886, several pictures, including the Ansidei Raphael, being acquired by the National Gallery.

On 9th October 1773 in his *Journal of a Tour to the Hebrides, with Samuel Johnson, LL.D.*, Boswell had written:

"Blenheim being occasionally mentioned, he told me he had never seen it: he had not gone formerly; and he would not put it in the power of some man about the Duke of Marlborough to say, 'Johnson was here; I knew him, but I took no notice of him!' He said, he should be very glad to see it, if properly invited, which in all probability would never be the case, as it was not worth his while to seek for it."

135. Jacob Bryant was secretary to the Duke and among the treasures he showed Johnson were:

Rationale Divinorum Officiorum, written by William Durand, Bishop of Mende, and first printed by Fust and Schoeffer at Mainz in 1459.

Lascaris's *Grammar*, the first book to be printed in Greek type.

The Battle of the Frogs and Mice; the first edition printed by Laonicus Cretensis at Venice in 1486.

136. John Coulson was a senior Fellow of University College and something of an eccentric.

137. Dr. Robert Vansittart was Regius Professor of Civil Law [See Mrs. Thrale's entry for 25 September].

Here Johnson's Diary ends. He stayed on in Oxford with the Thrales until 28th September when the party resumed the journey home, travelling via Benson and Crowmarsh to Edmund Burke's house, Gregories, at Beaconsfield. Here they received news of the Dissolution of Parliament on 30th September and left at once for London to start Henry Thrale's election campaign.

Journal of a Tour in Wales with Dr. Johnson

Mrs Thrale

On Tuesday, 5th July, 1774, I began my journey through Wales. We set out from Streatham in our coach and four post horses, accompanied by Mr. Johnson and our eldest daughter. Baretti[1] went with us as far as London, where we left him, and hiring fresh horses they carried us to the Mitre at Barnet, a house kept by Lady Lade's Maid,[2] with whom I left a letter for her quondam mistress. At St. Albans we were hospitably received by Ralph Smith[3] and his Wife, relations to Mr. Thrale, who gave us a good cold dinner and from whom we had much trouble to get away to a sister[4] of theirs who has another house in the Town, and detained us to drink tea with her and her son. There I was first made to observe the apparent degeneration of the wild pheasant's plumage when rendered domestic. In the afternoon we drove on to Dunstable, where we spent the night, after a day in which nothing else had been learned, seen, done, or known, but the passing through a space of 40 miles from home with emotions perpetually changing and perpetually strong, every sign, every bush, every stone almost, reminding me of times long past but not forgotten; of incidents not pleasing in themselves perhaps, but delightful from their connection with youthful gaiety and the remembrance of people now dead, to some of which I was far more dear than to any now living. Here I hunted with my Uncle, here I fished or walked with my Father, here my Grandmother reproved my Mother for her too great indulgence of me, here poor dear Lady Salusbury fainted in the coach and charged me not to tell Sir Thomas of the accident lest it should affect him, here we were overturned, and on this place I wrote foolish verses which were praised by my foolisher Friends.[5]

6th July. In the morning I went over to a house I had often been at, the house of Stokes, who was horse dealer to my Uncle, and there talk'd old times till Mr. Johnson, who had proposed rising at six, should himself be risen; this was about 10 o'clock, and we threatened to Inn at Meriden for the convenience of our attendants, who I think could not possibly have ridden to Lichfield, and I was in good hope that for their sakes we should have stopt short of Lichfield, which I well knew would be a heavy day's journey for my daughter, who had never travelled so long a way, nor scarce at all indeed since she was a baby. However, Mr. Thrale suggested the expedient of their being put in a post chaise, and the apparent preference of their convenience to mine, who had expressed my desire of shortening the journey, made me out of humour for the rest of the way, tho' I hope I gave nobody reason to perceive it. Mr. Johnson continued in good spirits, and often said how much pleasanter it was travelling by night than by day, &c. The clock struck 12 at Lichfield soon after we got in, and I had many feelings for Queeney which I was forced to suppress, as I was often told how little it signified whether she catch'd cold or no. She accordingly escaped with a slight cold and a sore eye.

[7th July.] In the morning of the next day I put off my riding dress and went down to the parlour of the Inn we slept at in a morning night gown and close cap, but Mr. Johnson soon sent me back to change my apparel for one more gay and splendid.[6] I acted accordingly, and was introduced in the first place to Mr. Greene, who has a small but curious collection of all natural and artificial rarities, particularly a Pulse Glass,[7] exhibiting the powers of rarefaction and condensation in a manner I never saw them exemplified before. Here I saw many things I never saw before, and came away with a catalogue in my pocket and some new images in my mind which the catalogue will at any time revive. The gentleman who entertained us with his curiosities appeared to have much knowledge and an officious earnestness to please which never fails of producing the effect intended where it is unaccompanied with Literature or *any* shining qualification, still more in a man whose eminence in his circle renders him somewhat of a respectable character. The Cathedral service, where an anthem was sung by Mr. Greene's directions for our entertainment, filled up an hour after dinner very properly. The Cathedral bears manifest marks of the devastation of the Fanatics, and contrary to their intent, these marks make it more venerable.[8] I saw Mr. Johnson's old house too,[9] which filled my mind with emotion, so tender and so pleasing, that I would have been sorry to quit it for the sake of seeing the Vatican till I had reiterated every image it gave me as often as I could feel the impression. We found Mrs. Lucy Porter at Cards with her friends in a pleasing house she has in the Town, where she received us very kindly and politely, showed us Mr. Johnson's picture and her Mother's, which I was exceedingly glad to have an opportunity of seeing it as Miss Porter said it was like. We finished the evening at Miss Aston's, upon Stow Hill. I thought there was some dignity and much oddity both in the mansion and the possessor, but she was very obliging to us all and seems to love Mr Johnson. She is a high-bred woman, quite the remains of an old beauty, lofty and civil at once.

[8th July.] The next morning began by breakfasting with Doctor Darwin, a Physician of this Town, who has an elegant house in it where he entertained us very kindly. We were then invited to see some East India rarities belonging to a Mr. Newton, who exhibited his curiosities with great willingness to oblige us; here I saw some Indian coins I had never seen before. At Dr. Darwin's there is a rose tree as tall as an apple tree and immensely full of flowers. I counted 100 and left so many untold that I was weary of conjecturing the numbers. Mr. Greene dined with us, and we drank tea with Mrs. Cobb at a curious old Friery where there are some painted glass panes, and I think the old Confessional still standing. Mr. Peter Garrick[10] supped with us at our Inn; the resemblance between him and his brother is so striking that I took the liberty to mention it. Mrs. Cobb said, Madam, they are the two Sosias.[11] He is still *more* like my poor Mother about the eyes, which our daughter and our servants observed as well as myself. Mr. Thrale went this day to the seat of Lord Donnegal[12] at Fisherwick, while I surveyed the fine things at Mr. Newton's. This was 8th July. Mr. Newton's collection of old Japan is by far the finest I ever yet have seen.

9th July. We left Lichfield, a place I had never seen before, and now had remained there only three days. I left it, however, with regret, such had been the kindness with which I had been both received and dismissed. I went early in the morning while my Gentlemen were dressing, to take leave of Miss Porter, whose superfluous attention flattered me exceedingly. We breakfasted with Mr. Garrick, who showed us every possible civility and waited on us at our Inn, where we parted with him and Mr. Greene, our other new Friend. It was now high time to set out for Sudbury, where we dined, and changing horses, went forward through a very fine Country to Doctor Taylor's at Ashbourne. My spirits were not high. Queeney breaks my heart and my head with her cough. I am scarce able to endure it. Dr. Taylor took possession of us very kindly, and we saw his pretty cascade, but it is not so pleasing as that of Town Malling.[13]

Sunday, 10th July. We went to the Church, where Dr. Taylor has a magnificent seat; indeed, everything around him is both elegant and splendid. He has very fine pictures which he does not understand the beauties of, a glorious Harpsichord which he sends for a young man out of the town to play upon, a waterfall murmuring at the foot of his garden, deer in his paddock, pheasants in his menagerie, the finest coach horses in the County, the largest horned cattle, I believe, in England, particularly a Bull of an enormous size, his table liberally spread, his wines all excellent in their kinds, his companions, indeed, are as they must be – such as the Country affords. We had a specimen of them today - very poor creatures both women and men. Queeney this day took a quarter of a Scot's Pill,[14] which I hoped would entirely carry off the cough which was going of its own accord, so she had a pretty comfortable night, and was disturbed by it but once.

On Monday, 11th, we were taken to Ilam Gardens,[15] a place of which I had heard much and from which of course I expected much, but it answered all my expectations and even surpassed them. A river rolls through the middle of a delightful valley formed by two very high rocks entirely covered with wood, which forms, as the phrase is, an amphitheatre; a hill, the basis of which is three miles in circumference and the height proportionate, fills up the end with great propriety, and looks majestically up the whole. This is all the garden, and this produces more surprise and more delight in the beholder than all the ornaments of all the gardens in the Nation. The day was warm and wet, so my poor Queeney soaked her feet completely up to her mid-leg; it rained all the while we were there, and she had her cough upon her, though not otherwise indisposed. I took off her shoes and stockings, however, in Mr. Port's House, where the servants as well as the master were ready and attentive. We got them quite dry again too or very near, and I half flattered myself she had not increased her cold, but the night told another story. She waked at 2 o'clock and coughed till 3, again at 5 o'clock and coughed till 6. She kept up her spirits, however, and her general health, eat, and ran, and laughed as usual, and was impatient for to-morrow's adventures.

12th July. Dr. Taylor took us to Chatsworth, where I was pleased with scarcely anything. The cascade is too artificial to satisfy an eye accustomed as one is in this Country to see water falling with rapidity from real rocks and swallowed up at last by real rivers. The other waterworks are bawbles fit only to amuse Boarding School Misses by wetting their playfellows' clothes. After seeing Ilam Gardens all gardens sink in your opinion, and the house is inferior in magnificence, convenience, and propriety of ornament to many that I have seen. We slept at a wretched Inn at Edensor, where, however, Hetty had the best night she has experienced since her cold. She slept without interruption from half-past 8 to half-past 4. The rest of the morning she coughed indeed, but she was now all alive and able to bear it. Never was so noisy nor I think so disgustful a lodging. I dairst hardly venture to bed at all, there were so many rude, drunken people about, but Queeney lay quieter than she has done these two or three nights.

[13th July.] On the morrow we drove to Matlock Bath,[16] where Dr. Taylor, who is well known and respected by all the people of the Country, introduced us to Mr. Abney[17] and Mr. Okeover, two pretty young gentlemen who have estates hard by, and Mr. Okeover engaged us all to dine with him tomorrow. Matlock consists, like Mr. Port's garden, of a rock, a wood, and a river, but there is a wider river and a steeper rock at Matlock than at Ilam. We climbed the rock, however, and ferried over the river, dined with the company at the public table, and admired the numberless beauties of the place, which I believe have now fairly exhausted the memory to describe and the language to express. The craggs, however, increased upon us and the streams gushed thro' more fissures as we passed forward to the Cotton Mill of a Mr. Arckwright,[18] whose ingenuity in the contrivance of his machines is as striking a curiousity as any we have been called to contemplate. The triumphs of Art and of nature are surely all exhibited in Derbyshire. To this work we were attended by our new friends Okeover and Abney, who appear to like us. I should mention a displeasing circumstance which happened at Matlock while I was there. A poor Girl who sold cherries to the Company was half run over and greatly hurt by a post chaise suddenly and briskly driving by. Well! from Mr. Arckwright's we drove on to Ashbourne, which I now call home, such is Dr. Taylor's hospitality and kindness, and here I can nurse my Niggey, whose cough seems to have gained new strength, though I cannot guess why, for the day has been remarkably fine, the first fair day indeed since we left Surrey, and I had like to have forgot to record it, though I threatened so often to do so.

[14th July.] Queenie had a miserable night this night, and so of course had I. I sat up with her till 3, her fever was quite high till then, and after that she sweat a good deal and was better again in the morning. I gave her a large dose of Glauber's Salts, which procured her more ease than all I had hitherto done, and this I ventured though we were engaged to dine at Okeover, where we sate down twenty-two people to dinner. Here I saw the famous picture supposed to be Raphael's, for which the possessor, Mr. Okeover, has been offered £1400. It is a Holy Family, in fine preservation, and eminently excellent. This served as a topic for talk, which, however, grew difficult to diversify, and the evening went off heavily, tho' every effort for amusement was made. We saw Mr. Okeover's Chapel. The ladies fingered his organ, and smart things were said concerning a monument set up by some Widower with a winged Hymen quenching his Torch. In the evening we came home, so we now call Ashbourne, and here I am sitting to my journal by my daughter's bedside trying to flatter myself that her cough mends. This is Thursday, 14th July, 1774.

[15th July.] She had a shocking night, however, and till between 4 and 5 in the morning never settled to sleep. I got some rest then myself, and to my much astonishment when we rose for the day she had almost entirely lost her cough. This day 15th July we were visited by the Dyott family; the gentlemen drank, the ladies sang and played on the Doctor's fine Harpsichord, while Mr. Thrale rode over to see Meynell's Foxhounds,[19] which he said were very fine ones. In the afternoon Mr. Johnson took me to drink tea with a relation of his, a Mrs. Flint who lives in this town and has a daughter so like my poor Lucy that it brought tears to my eyes. The pretty creature also is strangely tormented with headaches. I was quite shocked at the hearing of it. I called in likewise upon my old friend Mrs. Hayne and her sister Mrs. Heathcote, Mrs. Hayne's name is Dale now. They were at dinner but *so* glad to see me again forsooth that I promised to spend another hour with them before I leave Ashbourne. On this night Queeney made herself good amends for all her sleepless nights. She went to bed at 9 and never stirred till 12, when she coughed three times and I feared we were all to begin again, but in a quarter of an hour it was over, and the lady waked no more till the clock had struck 8 in the morning. I think this anxiety is *now* fairly over.

16th July. We spent this morning in surveying the beauties of Dovedale[20] in company with a Mr. Langley, a Schoolmaster of this town and well skilled in the art of showing the antiquities and curiosities of the place, a Mr. Gilpin and his Friend Parker, who are young men travelling about England for pleasure and improvement; and Mr. Flint, Dr. Taylor's dependent, who went with us instead of the Doctor who was particularly engaged. These gentlemen waited on Mr. Johnson, Mr. Thrale, my daughter, and myself, who clambered the rocks with real satisfaction, as every step varied the view, and filled my mind with pictures which will not easily be erased. Every thing that this wild Country boasts is united in Dovedale, where the elegance of Ilam and the steep of Matlock are both outdone, the river too is more exquisitely clear and pellucid than I have yet seen water even in Derbyshire, where you cannot travel a mile without hearing a gushing stream either gliding over smooth stones or rattling over rough ones. The craggs in Dovedale are the largest I ever yet saw, or at least remember, the rock facing Reynard's Hall is particularly grand, and the prospect of the opposite mountain through the arch eminently pleasing. One particular place where the river is very narrow and rocks nearer together than in any other part, Mr. Langley called the Streights, and there Mr. Johnson observed that one might build a Summer House with great convenience upon an arch over the stream uniting the opposite hills. Our servant Sam caught a Blackbird in one of the caverns, but we let it go again. We were shown the precipice down which Dean

Langton fell and bruised himself to death. We were likewise shown another precipice the sight of which so frightened somebody that she fainted at the view, and must have fallen headlong had not a gentleman present caught hold of her suddenly and saved her life. The only thing wanting to the effect Dovedale has on a spectator is water. The river Dove is too narrow a stream for the rocks. The rocks are worthy to stand on the banks of the Po, and this river is neither deep nor broad; it is, however, the clearest of all rivulets and makes a sweet murmuring in the valley. The evening of this day I spent with my two old friends Mrs. Dale and Mrs. Heathcote, where I heard and talked a thousand old stories and reciprocated some kindness and of course some pleasure. Queeney's cough is now not worth thinking on, she has a slight touch of the worms too, but I don't much mind that; we shall do very well, I believe, but 'tis so melancholy a thing to have nobody one can speak to about one's clothes, or one's child, or one's health, or what comes uppermost. Nobody but *Gentlemen*, before whom one must suppress everything except the mere formalities of conversation and by whom every thing is to be commended or censured. Here my paper is blistered with tears for the loss of my companion, my fellow traveller, my Mother, my friend, my attendant, who packed my trunks and eased all my cares, while her conversation enlivened one's mind and her observations on every thing were thought well of by the wisest. I hoped, and very vainly hoped that wandering about the World would lessen my longing after her, but who now have I to chat with on the Road? who have I to tell my adventures to when I return? Every place I see, every thing I hear recalls my Mother and rekindles my concern.

17th July was Sunday and we went to Church. Some ladies came to dinner and we spent the evening drinking tea with Mrs. Dyott's family, where nothing extraordinary happened. At dinner today, however, a family history was related which struck me greatly. There lives somewhere in this neighbourhood a Country Gentleman of £200 a year estate.[21] This man had two wives and three sons. To his eldest was bequeathed an estate of £1500 a year lately with an injunction to take the name of Okeover in respect to his Great Uncle who made the bequest. His second is now in actual possession of £2000 a year left him by a Godfather no ways related to him, and the third son who is by the second wife will have Sir Edward Lyttelton's whole estate and fortune in right of his Mother, who was his Niece. The first of these young men is our friend Okeover, at whose house we dined.

18th July. We dined at Mr. Gell's after paying a morning visit to Mr. Alsop.

Never did my aversion rise so suddenly and in such high tides as towards that Mr. Gell. A man visibly impaired by age and particularly ugly, talking largely and loudly on every subject, understanding none as I could find, foppish without elegance, confident without knowledge, sarcastic without wit and old without experience, a man uniting every hateful quality, a deist, a dunce, and a cotquean.[22] This man six weeks ago married an ignorant girl in the neighbourhood not yet sixteen years old, and ours was a wedding visit. The girl was a gentlewoman, it seems, with a pretty face enough and a decent fortune. The jest is that she loves this fellow apparently and unaffectedly, I think loves him as entirely as her poor little narrow mind can be capable of loving any one. So here ends the character of the Gells with whom we spent this day.

19th July. We rose earlier than usual to go to Kedlestone and Derby, at the last of which places we proposed to dine and return to Doctor Taylor in the evening. We saw Kedlestone therefore, and saw there more splendor of furniture and more ostentation of wealth than I have ever yet seen in any house ancient or modern. The pictures are of high value, the state apartments grand beyond expectation and beyond description. I think no house I have seen at all comparable to this of Lord Scarsdale for finery, neither are the ornaments of a tinsel taste; there is intrinsic value in the glitter of this gay mansion. There is, however, no pleasing disposition of well-contrived apartments, no elegance of proportion nor no happy introduction of light to be boasted of, nothing but what so much money might buy, and what would apparently sell for so much money again. A printed catalogue of the sculpture and paintings was put into my hand; here I read Claude *Lorenze* for Claude *Lorraine*, and here Mr. Johnson corrected some gross anachronism I forget what, but when you mount up to the attic story the scene is so altered it frights you, such low rooms, and so gloomy that they form a strong contrast to the gayety of the showy apartments downstairs. After our eyes had been dazzled below and deadened above we drove on to Derby, where we saw the silk mills. Here I learned the reason why the Chinese Ribbands are so called; some China silk perfectly untwisted was woven for that purpose and succeeded very well. The ribbons are of an exquisite softness, though I am told the China silk is far from being the best or the finest. Bengal silk is likewise of an inferior quality, the Italian is the best in all respects, and that from Pezaro [Pesaro] the first among the Italians. I should have heard more of such matters but that the stench of the place was so oppressive it made me quite sick and I could scarcely speak to the man who showed the machines. All the mechanical parts of this exhibition are better performed by Mr. Arckwright's Cotton Mill near Matlock. We stole an hour in the forenoon of this day to visit

Mr. Meynell's Kennel which contains the most complete pack of Foxhounds I ever yet saw.

20th July. We took leave of Dr.Taylor and of Ashbourne, a place where we received even superfluous civility, and a man of dignity enough to make that civility valuable. The Doctor appears to a cursory spectator one of the happiest of the human race, with knowledge enough to employ some solitude, and money enough to enjoy society – money indeed to purchase all the conveniences and even luxuries of life: Pictures, Musick, Books and Friends, besides a power over his neighbours, and an influence extended, as I understand, to no inconsiderable distance. This makes the great men near him look up, not down to him, and forces a respect which he is willing enough to receive. Between ambition and indolence, however, this man is preserved from being an object of envy; to secure his power he is obliged to gratify his dependants sometimes to the pejorating his fortune by suffering tenants to live at low rents, and sometimes chusing his companions according to the caprices and prejudices of a few who can command votes on the day of a general election. On the whole he is a man whom one would wish to please, and a man whom one would expect to be more pleasing when removed from his own circle to a wider range of company and conversation. We left him at eleven o'clock and drove to Buxton,[23] which I found more agreeable than I expected; the Bath was wonderfully delightful. I could not resist the temptation of going in for a quarter of an hour, but I was weary of it then and found it relaxed me too much for mere pleasure. We prosecuted our journey over precipices and heaths and came late to Macclesfield, where I saw the finest Pear tree (nailed to a wall) that ever I saw in my life.

21st July. We continued our journey towards Combermere through a fertile but displeasing country, the roads being heavy and the views confined. The salt works and springs at Namptwick amused us, however, and the Innkeeper told us that there used to be annual merry-makings in honour of those curiosities, but the custom was now left off.[24] They did not omit in their mirth to thank the Giver of all Good for their peculiar felicity he said, for they always began and ended their merriment with – "Oh ye Fountains and Wells, bless ye the Lord, praise him and magnify him for ever." The next stage brought us to Sir Lynch S. Cotton's, where we were kindly received and splendidly treated.

22nd July. We spent the morning in rowing on the Mere and examining the Island where a summer house stands very agreeably in view of the house, which is in all respects better than I expected to find it. What most surprised me, however, is my disposition to like everything here, and it sometimes produces reflexions I would rather be free from. While my Mother lived who half adored the whole family, I was perpetually finding if not seeking opportunities of magnifying their absurdities and defects; now I perceive myself willing to excuse them and content to think as well of them as they will let me. This disposition, whatever it proceeds from, proceeds not from good I fear; however, as it cannot tend towards evil, it may as well be indulged.

23rd July. This day we took horse and rode to Lord Kilmorey's Seat at Shevington [Shavington] six miles off. The house has nothing in it to be remembered, as it is merely commodious within and of decent appearance without, but wholly devoid of elegance or splendour. The owner, however, is a character as the phrase is. A man who, joining the bluster of an Officer to the haughtiness of a Nobleman newly come to his estate – an estate which had held his Soul in suspense perhaps for twenty years – endeavours to swell the gay Jack Needham into the magnificent Lord Kilmorey, and is to me a man extremely offensive. His severity is mere clownishness, his civilities carry an air of condescension no way pleasing, and his general behaviour is so turgid that if one is not shocked at it, one must be diverted. So absurdly triumphant too, comparing his house with Keddlestone, his estate with Lord Scarsdale's, and his pool with Sir Lynch Cotton's Lake. All that he said and did, even his politeness, excited and promoted disgust.[25]

24th July. On this day we heard Divine Service performed in a Chapel my Uncle built about a mile from the house at Burleydam, where stood an old tattered place unfit for the purpose. It is a neat plain edifice and the Communion Plate of suitable value. Sir Lynch says the whole cost him six hundred pounds, but I know not how far he is to be believed. He showed me some old women that my Mother had known formerly, and I fretted at having no money in my pocket, but I will see them again. There is a picture of my Mother here which we used to laugh at for being so unlike, and now I fancy I see a resemblance. What an odd thing is the human mind! We are to rise early tomorrow to view Sir Rowland Hill's fine house and grounds. I had written so far of my Journal when I went to chat with my Uncle in his little room, and found the family in great confusion, the youngest daughter being this very morning married to a young fellow in the house, son of their friend Colonel D'Avenant.[26] Mr. Thrale and Mr. Johnson lent their assistance to pacify the Parents and smooth the objections, but as great wrath is expected from the young gentleman's Father and Mother the new married couple agreed to go off For Chester in their road to Llewenny this evening, and Miss Cotton and I rode with them as far as Whitchurch, then we had to come home in the dark almost. This journey was happily performed and no accident happened however. Tomorrow we go to this Hawkestone.

25th July. Sir Rowland Hill's place is so fine it must begin a fresh side all to itself. The situation is extremely favourable for the disposition of grounds in a sublime taste, lofty, craggy, woody, not fringed with bushes to conceal its barrenness, but ornamented with timber trees of a considerable height and size. The rocks are really formidable, not made the most of to excite ideas of terror, but truly dangerous to Climb, and not very docile when cut into seats, the rudeness of which exceeds anything I ever saw, many of them having no paths made to them, and seeming at a distance wholly inaccessible. From these seats, however, the most striking prospects are to be seen; all the rough crags of Hawkestone, with whole promontorys of woodland stretching out into the beautiful meadows that compose the valley below, fill up the foreground. When the eye is tempted further a country of long extent and high cultivation detains it from the Welsh mountains, which, lying at a great distance, terminates the prospect. Shrewsbury looks particularly beautiful from one of the seats and the Staffordshire hills have a fine effect from another. The grotto is spacious and well contriv'd, with agreeable intricacies and artless pillars, rudely hewn out of the natural rock, which suggested the orginal idea. There are some ornaments of spar, shells, &tc., but there is no foppery in them, nor are they injudiciously crowded. Upon the whole I consider Hawkestone as a place of the first class in this Kingdom and never cease astonishing myself that it has escaped pompous description. As words, however, are but poor representations of things I do not much regret the loss of such reputation as words could give. This is a place which should be seen, and when it is seen is sure to be admired. As nothing, however, is quite complete, so Hawkstone has no water near it, but a mean canal which were better away.

26th July. On this day we took our leave of Combermere where we had been very kindly treated. I left them, too, liking them better than ever I liked them, though Sir Lynch's rusticity and his Wife's emptiness afforded nothing but a possibility of change from disgust to insipidity. The marriage of young

D'Avenant with Miss Hetty made the most amusement for us all. Something to consult about, something to talk of, which it is the great misery of unintellectual people constantly to want. However, we have now left them and are come to Chester. The Wall is a wonderful work I think, but as it is now wholly useless, is so totally neglected and forgotten that as one walks upon it one thinks – since neither strength, nor bulk nor antiquity suffice to reserve anything from oblivion let us endeavour to be useful that we too may not be forgotten.

27th July. On this day we perambulated the City, but with more haste than attention.[27] I saw various objects amongst which was the Cathedral, where I thought the singing below indifferent, and which is of itself a mean edifice adorned in the Gothic taste, but its appearance so fresh, that it seemed more like imitation than reality. The altar piece being Tapestry[28] only, gives a poverty of look to the whole, and it is altogether the poorest Cathedral I have yet seen. The Chapter House, however, which is likewise a Library, has a venerable air, and the Cloysters have as much dignity of aspect as [any] I have seen.

28th July. On this day we took leave of Chester, and Cheshire and England, and proceeded to Wales. I must not, however, quit the Nation though but for a week, and be content wholly to forbear mentioning one place and one person who deserves more notice than almost any of the places or persons I have been more ready to remember. I mean Poole's Hole in Derbyshire for the place, and Miss Hill of Hawkstone for the Person. Poole's Hole, indeed, I have no right to describe, for I only went in so far that I could easily find my way out again, and the curiosity of this cavern chiefly consists in the size of it. It was, however, gloomy and lofty where I saw it, very chill just at the entrance, but warmer when one was got a little way. The petrefactions, too, hanging down in odd figures, seemed ornaments perfectly suitable to the solemnity of the place, where imaginative people might dress up a thousand ideas of horror, but cool examination could, I think, find little except disgust. In the *Lady* too, that I had forgotten to record, there is an odd mixture of sublimity and meanness. Her conversation is elegant, her dress uncommonly vulgar, her manner lofty if not ostentatious, and her whole appearance below that of a common house-maid. She is, however, by far the most conversible Female I have seen since I left home, her character, I hear, is respectable, and her address is as polite as can be wished. I shall never see her again probably, and I am sorry for it. One could wish to see her very often.

29th July. Yesterday evening we came into Llewenny, which struck me extremely as an old family seat of no small dignity. Superfluous space seems to be one source of satisfaction in a house, and here is a hall and a gallery which never seem intended for use, but merely stateliness of appearance. The Gallery is exactly 75 of my steps to the end. In our way to this place we stopt for refreshment at Mold, where we examined the Church, and observed a monument erected by some foolish fellow to *himself* professing his dislike of flattery.[29] The Country we passed through is of peculiar beauty, and I saw no mountains but what were cultivated to the top, which was never, as I could see, higher than the South Downs of Sussex. This morning we were to have gone over to Bachygraig, but such was the weather that it was impossible to stir out, at least for ladies, so Mr. Thrale stole a march upon me and went with Mr. Cotton. He said at his return that it was better than he expected. Tomorrow we shall see.

30th July. I went to see my possessions, which I found far worse than I had expected. The house less spacious and the woods less thick. In the house, however, are three excellent rooms, over which there seems little else but pigeon-holes in a manner peeping out of the roof, and at the top of all a ridiculous Lanthorn with a ladder to get up to it. The picture of the Children of Israel bitten by serpents did not equal my idea of it, but I should think that and

The stable-block at Lleweni Hall.

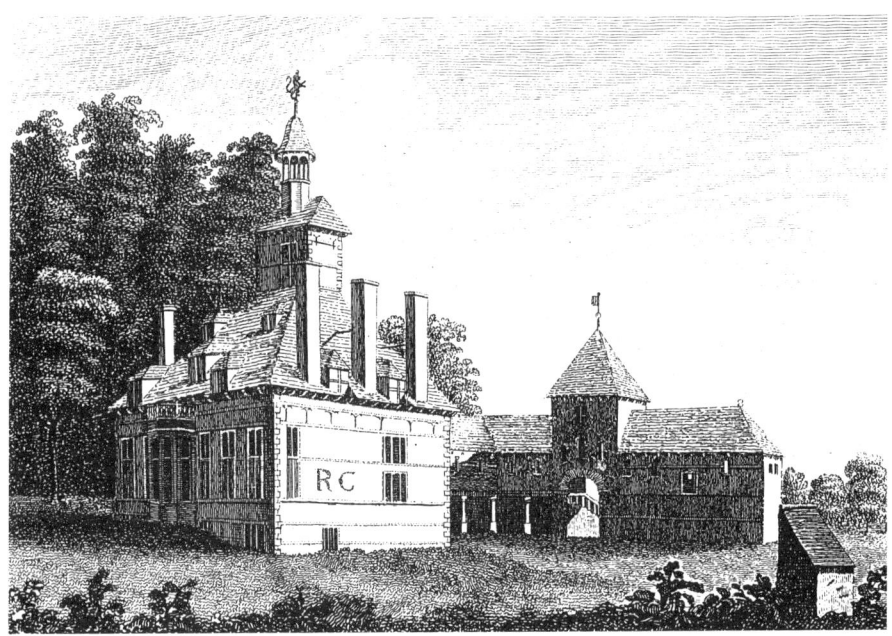

Above: Bachygraig in 1776.

Below: The 16th century barn at Bachygraig.

its companion over the chimney might be worth something too, with a Ecce Homo upon wood that really appears capital. The walls of the house and the roof of it have, I think, solidity enough to last some centuries, and such is the situation that the place might really be made delightful if one pleased. The lawn would be easily stretched down to the river, which rolls at the foot of a meadow in front of the house, and there is a bridge built by Inigo Jones of a single arch that faces the door. Woods shelter the back front on each side, through which very pleasing walks might soon be cut, and towards this front all the good rooms look unluckily, for before the house there is as fine a country as I ever have seen in my life. A gatehouse, however, placed straight before the front door impedes all possibility of view, and the warehouses on the side, however useful, are far from being ornaments to the whole. I really think if the top was taken off and a story of decent rooms built in their stead, the house might yet be convenient and fit for a family. We rode over a part of the estate which is said to be good, and I think it really seems so; the corn fields are surrounded with deep hedge rows planted with oak, which are said to stretch their shade so as to hinder the approach of the sun and prevent the growth of the grain. There is a great deal more wood than I thought when I first saw it.

Sunday, 31st July. Today we heard Divine Service at St. Asaph Cathedral, where the singing was very miserable indeed, but the choir was less mean than I apprehended it would be, and the general look of the Church was really respectable, very little below Chester Cathedral, if at all. The Dean preached and the Bishop gave us his blessing. His Lordship invited us all to his Palace, which, as he said, would be a good creditable Parsonage House in any of the less remote Counties. His Wife gave us Cakes and Currants, pressed us to stay dinner, and was as civil as she knew how, but she is a vulgar woman,[30] and indeed I never saw a Spiritual Lord who had a genteel Wife. The reason is evident. They are commonly mean men raised by Scholarship to the rank of a Bishop, but as they marry in their youth, they marry to their equals, and the woman, who never rises in her behaviour, as the man often enough contrives to do, grows only more disagreeable as her situation in life gives her more opportunities of displaying herself. So much for the Bishop and his Lady.

Monday, 1st August. We were taken to see Denbigh Castle, the situation of which I think surpasses Clifden [Cliveden] for gayety and beauty. Thro' every arch or hole in the wall some gentleman's house or some elegant ornamental building or some solemn wood or some cultivated hill whose gentle rise seems contrived on purpose to shew the enclosures on its side, are discovered, and each view is called the most beautiful till another is examined. The Castle is strong, the arch finely proportioned, and the effigies of the Earl of Lincoln on the top not much defaced. The ivy has given one side more the appearance of a hedge than a wall, and the *tout ensemble*, as the Dilettants phrase it, is too delicately pleasing to afford one any of the images one expects from an old castle. Upon the whole it looks like a ruin built on purpose, in the midst of a delightful garden belonging to a man of exquisite taste, not like that which the imagination makes for its own amusement when solitude encourages the frolicks of fancy. In our return from this place we saw Whitchurch, where, as at all Churches in this valley, lights are kindled at 2 in the morning on every Xmas Day, and songs of joy and genuine gratitude are accompanied by the Harp and resound to the cottages below, whose little inhabitants rousing at the call hasten and chuse a convenient place to dance till prayer time, which begins at sunrise and separates the dancers for a while.[31]

Tuesday, 2nd August. Mr. Cotton took us today to his Summer-house in the Wood, from whence we had a fine view of the vale, and then rode on to Dymerchion my Parish Church, where many of my progenitors, particularly my Father, lye buried;[32] many more indeed we trampled over yesterday when we looked at an Abbey[33] of which little now remains, just below the Castle of Denbigh, and which is the property of Mr. Cotton of Llewenny. The Church at Dymerchion is in a dismal condition, the seats all tumbling about, the Altar rail falling, the vessels for the consecrated elements only pewter, the cloth upon the table in a thousand holes, and the floor strewed with rushes. Of the seats, however, wretched as they are, my family possesses fourteen, and these the best. The poor Clerk addressed me with the saying of Simeoń, Lord, now lettest thou, etc., since he had seen me he said he should die in peace. I was shocked at the man. From hence we went to Llanerch, the seat of Mr. Davies, with elegant grounds and a very pleasing piece of water about it. I took the more interest in its appearance as I had often heard my Mother say that was the house in Wales where she had spent the happiest hours. She loved the late Mrs. Davies dearly.

Wednesday, 3rd August. On this day we were carried to Holywell, where we saw the devastation committed by Puritanism, which in its zeal had battered poor Saint Winifred and displaced her statue, broken three of the columns surrounding the Well which had any effigies upon them, and left nothing but the stone at the bottom of the water which bears any mark of ancient superstition and is spotted with red in two or three places, and the Roman Catholics believe from their hearts that it was stained by the blood of their favourite Virgin martyr. The spring is so clear and pellucid that it tempts one to jump into it, but the wonder is in the thoughts of its throwing up 100 tun in a minute. When you look, however, at the rapidity with which the water throws itself off, you wonder no longer, and are willing to believe on the spot that which at a distance seemed wholly incredible. The stream turns 19 Mills, and is of prodigious use to the Copper Works below, over which we walked and observed the Lapis Calaminaris in its natural state. I had likewise an opportunity of seeing what I have always known but never seen, the cutting of a bar of iron at a stroke and the heat which that strong friction occasions. One could, however, scarcely forbear laughing at the reflection that we were all so well content to be gaping 200 miles from Streatham at what we might see every day two miles from our own door. Thoyts's Copper Mill at Merton[34] is doubtless as curious as the works at Holywell, but we came hither to wonder, so let us wonder away.

Thursday, 4th August. We went to Ruhdlan [Rhuddlan] Castle, a place very different from Denbigh. Wild in its situation, rude in its appearance, the haunt of screaming gulls and clamourous rooks, a magazine below it which serves as a beacon to ships liable to suffer distress in their dangerous passage across the Irish Seas. Barren rocks rising on one side and the sea roaring on the other fill the mind with poetical imagery. Images of captivity, courage, or desperation. Here Danae might have been immured, here Andromeda might have been exposed, and here Alcyone might have breathed her last on the corpse of the faithful Coyx [Ceyx].[35] From this place Mrs. Cotton was half unwilling to move, she had so often wandered in the recesses of the castle which had been the play places of her youth, Mr. Johnson told her that her sisters and she should agree to fortify it against their husbands and resolve to stand the siege with spirits. Hence, however, we drove on to Bodryhdan [Bodryddan][36] where we saw an agreeable place hastening to decay for want of a male heir, and here I thanked God that he had *given me two sons.* Desurt [Dyscrth] Cascade was the next object of our attention and it is the finest I have yet ever seen, falls from a greater height and has a break in the middle that is so pleasing one can scarce think it natural. At our return I went to see a poor woman who lyes ill in the neighbourhood, when feeling for my purse I perceived that I had lost it; it contained seven guineas and a half and four shillings. This was the first time I have been out of humour since Queeney got well of her cough, and this did so grieve me that I really could hardly suppress, much less conceal my emotion.

Gwaynynog: the South Front.

Friday, 5th August, was spent at Gwaynynog, a gentleman's house hard by, which had been a small one, I believe, but was enlarged of late as the family became prosperous. Here I first saw a company of genuine Welch folks, and cannot boast the elegance of the society. The women were vastly below the men in proportion, their manners were gross, and their language more contracted. The men, however, were not drunk nor the women inclined to disgrace themselves. I observe if there is an Officer in company they call him Mr. Captain, or Mr. Captain Cotton, which I never heard before. The dinner was splendid and we had ices in the desert.[37] The brother of the gentleman who invited us sent Mr. Thrale a Pine [pineapple] the day before, and I have reason to think the entertainment was made merely for us. Mr. Johnson's fame has penetrated *thus* far, and Mr. Myddleton said he had never before had so great a man under his roof, that he was perfectly sensible of the honour done him, etc.

Saturday, 6th August. Today we have company at home, as indeed we have almost every day. This is a place of great society and of tolerable good humour, I mean that I hear few family histories to the disgrace of the people spoken of, few things said maliciously, and few provokingly. I like the Country much, and if the inhabitants were better taught, one should like them too.

Sunday, 7th August. This was Church day, of course, and so we went to Bodvary, where, when the Parson saw us, he gave out that service should be performed in English. We had neither singing nor preaching, but it was Sacrament Sunday, and I saw to my surprise that the vessels were all of silver. Texts, some Welch, some English, were strewed about the Church, which was really below many a stable for convenience or beauty.

Monday, 8th August. This day the Bishop and his family dined here, Mr. Yonge of Acton and all his family were here before. I counted 24 people at tea; we dined in separate rooms. Mr. Cotton seems to live very hospitably, rather in my own opinion splendidly, but his neighbours who should know best seem to think differently of him. I believe he is a man who obstinately resists imposition, and declares it his intention to clear the estate by frugality and diligence. Such a person will perhaps always be thought niggardly in his neighbourhood, and would indeed be called a covetous fellow if he gave away £500 a year, and saw that it was given. The lady is a most amiable being, charitable, compassionate, modest, and gentle to a degree, almost unequalled by any woman whose want of fortune, person, or understanding did not set her apparently below her husband. She is, however, proportionately equal to him in both knowledge and riches, but so pliant, so tender, so attentive to his health, his children, and expenses, that I sincerely think of all the people I ever yet knew – he is the *happiest* in a Wife. *Sua si bona norint.*[38]

Tuesday, 9th August. I expected letters from home and had nonc[.] I have not Mrs. Cotton's even sweetness of temper, so I am come into my own room to cry. She loves her children as well as I do, but she would not have cried from fretful impatience like me. Why does every body on some occasion or other perpetually do better than I can?

Dr. Johnson's Urn, Gwaynynog.

Wednesday, 10th August. We dined at Maesmynnaw [Maesmynnan], where lives a Mr. Lloyd who is agent to half the gentlemen of the County and has a great desire to be mine. His daughter, an awkward wench, presided at the table, where everything, however, was elegantly served. The man makes great court to this family, and his son seems to be almost a part of it both at Combermere and here. Mr. Thrale seems to like him too. Maesmynnaw is a house of Sir Roger Mostyn's which Lloyd rents. The situation of it and the views from the windows are very pleasing. But the habitation is scarcely to be called of the second rate. There was obstreperous merriment among the men, yet I saw none of them drunk when they came to tea, and we all returned home in very good time as could be, the servants sober and the mistress too. I wondered! but the world is greatly civilized these late 15 or 20 years, and they drink ale too, so they might still make their company merry at a small expense if the cost of the wine was the sole reason of their forbearance, as Mr. Johnson has sometimes hinted.

Thursday, 11th August. I begged of Mr. D'Avenant[39] to go with me to Pentryffeth [Pontruffyd] when I paid my respects to good old Mrs. Lloyd who used to be kind to me when I was a girl. She expressed a desire of seeing my husband, so I sent him in the afternoon to wait on her, and was pleased with an opportunity of obliging the good old lady. This is the first day we have dined

Maesmynnan.

here so few as twelve at table. To-day Niggey was naughty and severely mortified for her insolence by being complained of and made to cry before the Company. It depressed her spirits so that she cried all day long almost. Some of Sir Thomas's heirs breakfasted with us. I think the County swarms with 'em.

Friday, 12th August. This day Mr. Cotton and Mr. Thrale dined at the Assizes at Ruthyn [Ruthin], Mr. and Mrs. D'Avenant went thither to the Ball, and Mrs. Cotton, Mr. Johnson, Queeney, and I were left all alone, and dined alone and talked. Mr. Johnson does not value Mrs. Cotton as much as she deserves. I mentioned her sweetness of disposition. True, says he, but it is in her nature, and one thanks her no more for being sweet than a honeycomb.

Saturday, 13th August. Mr. Thrale rode out with Queeney and I. We went to Bridge's,[40] where I heard a marvellous tale about my Father, which I suspect was a lye. I saw his picture, however, and there is a likeness. In my Mother's there is none. Sir Thomas is a sad dawb, yet has a general resemblance. My Grandmother Cotton is very like, and I fancy her Father like, for it is like *her*. We went on to Bachygraig, but did not look over the pictures there as I intended. Bridge has the key. We came down thro' our own woods and fields, and the ride seemed to do Queeney good. She was not well yesterday, had a touch of the headache, and looked heavy about the eyes, yet without any other symptom of Worms.[41] I rather think it is her Thursday's affliction that produced the ill looks and seeming dejection. She took half a Scots Pill yesterday, however, which worked her this morn: and that perhaps has done more for her than the riding.

Sunday, 14th August. We heard Prayers at Bodvary, with a Welch second Lesson and Sermon. They would have indulged us with English, but we refused. The beauty Mrs. Parry[42] of Llanmaidr [Llanrhaeadr] dined here, and is so like Mrs. Bunbury's picture of Reynolds's[43] that if it was drawn for her it could not be more so. Queeney has a weight over her eyes today again. I hear Harry has had a black eye, and Ralph cuts his teeth with pain, but I have nobody to tell how it vexes me. Mr. Thrale will not be conversed with by *me* on any subject, as a friend, or comforter, or adviser. Every day more and more do I feel the loss of my Mother. My present Companions have too much philosophy for me. One cannot disburthen one's mind to people who are watchful to cavil, or acute to contradict before the sentence is finished.

Monday, 15th August. Mr. D'Avenant rode with me to Gwaynynog, and mounted Niggey on a little grey horse that carried her very cleverly. Mr. Myddleton was vastly polite and kind and invited us to his house in our return from Llyn or Llene [Lleyn],[44] so they all agree to call Caernarvonshire and Merionethshire. I suppose they know why. The woods of Gwaynynog are of peculiar beauty, hanging on each side the river from hills very lofty though sloping, and easy of ascent, as well as elegant in appearance. Nature has done all here that is done at Ilam, but the owner has made his walk through the wood near the top, not upon the lawn by the river side as at Mr. Port's. The water here too runs more rapidly than at Ilam, but then it is neither so clear nor so broad; in a word, the woods of Gwaynynog might at any time be trimmed up like the gardens of Ilam, and the gardens at Ilam being left untouch'd for a twelvemonth would resemble the walks of the Welchman. Seats, Cottages, and mottoes interspersed among the woods, have to my mind no unpleasing effect, tho' I have heard them censured as foppish, and foppish I think they are. The gentleman of this house is surely overfond of them. He talked to me of poor Dr. Goldsmith[45] and – now in Company, Madam (said he), was he *always* the great man? No, Sir, replied I, I think he was *never* the great man. We had more conversation about him, however, and I hope I did not do the dear Doctor injustice. I was wet thro' my shoes and stockings and habit, but Niggey saved herself from almost all the rain by running. I had made Sam carry her shoes and stockings for change in his pocket, so she came dry enough home, and I hope has caught no cold. She is better again today, but then she took physick last night, so I don't know yet whether it is the riding, or the evacuation that mends her, but she is certainly better tonight for some reason or other. I have the horrors whenever she has the headache.[46] God restore her looks and my peace again.

16th August. Queeney rose in such spirits that I fretted at myself for fretting about her, but she is always in spirits in the morning and at night and seems to flag in the middle of the day, so I think did poor Lucy. Oh! what a horrid thought; and she is feverish too, and hot in the hand. I wish I knew what ailed her. Nothing seen or heard today leaves melancholy thoughts too much liberty. I gave her some Salts today to cool her. The Aloes, I believe, were too hot physick.

17th August. I took leave of the poor sick woman and resolved to set off tomorrow in quest of fresh adventures. Adieu, Llewenny! I do not often delight myself much with people or with places, but Llewenny is a place, and Mrs.

Cotton a person, that I like extremely, and with whom I lived quite at my ease, and very much to my liking. I am half sorry to go, and to go on still further and further from home, yet if Queeney should be well, what should hinder our doing well, and receiving amusement? and to be sure every body does wonder why I think her sick, but so it was with Lucy. All the World thought her well but me, and I was right, God help me. But farewell, Llewenny, and farewell, dismal thoughts.

18th August. We set off much too late for Conway, where we arrived just at the time of the Races, where all the Country seemed to be collected, and beds could not be procured, so we were obliged to take the benefit of the full moon and push for Bangor over Penmanmawr, which answered all my expectations and was indeed the tremendous rock I have heard it was. One cannot say anything of the views as it was too dark to see them. The accommodations at Bangor were very bad; poor Mr. Johnson got only a share of some men's room, and the woman of the house proposed that he should sleep with Mr. Thrale and Queeney and I, who were all stuffed in one filthy room.

19th August. She called me up early, and I wandered on the 19th in the morning with her to the Cathedral,[47] which is lighter and better kept in repair than that of St. Asaph. But the seats, pulpit, etc. are all new, and have nothing that interests you. There is a Library, they say, but the key has long been lost I fancy, for nobody pretended to know where it was to be found. In this Churchyard I first saw a grave stuck with various flowers, a large bunch of Rosemary in the middle. As I was returning to breakfast at the Inn I spyed Mr. Thrale standing at a gentleman's door with the master of the house. He invited us in, lamented our ill accommodation, and promised us beds at his house for tonight. We accepted his kindness, and he ordered his Boat to Sea, and accompanied us to Beaumaris, where he sent for the Schoolmaster to show us the curiosities of the place. The Schoolmaster claimed acquaintance with Mr. Johnson, and we walked together with our new friends to Baron Hill, the seat of Lord Bulkeley, a place of beautiful situation commanding the Castle, the streights, and the mountains, an assemblage scarcely to be mended even by the imagination. We spent some time among the woods and the walks, and proceeded to a Castle of no small dignity or extent, yet much unknown to the talking World. Fifteen towers adorn and fortify the outer walls, the inner consists of eight only; but there is a Chapel here in such high preservation, as the phrase is, that one wonders. The goats browzed upon the grass, the ivy added solemnity to the ruin, and the whole filled one's eyes with pleasure, and one's mind with respect for those who edified and those who inhabited so fine a fortification. The gentleman was desirous of shewing Mr. Johnson his School, and so he did, and we rowed back to our good hospitable Mr. Roberts, whose Wife gave us her best tea, and lodged us in her best beds.

20th August. We put our pretty boat to sea again and spent some very agreeable hours on the water. The first thing that attracted our notice was Plasnewydd, the seat of Sir Nicholas Bayley,[48] a place of no small dignity and great convenience. The situation is peculiarly delightful. On the banks of the Streight, raised by terraces so as to secure it from damp and adorned by woods which shelter it on every side but the front. Here was a Chapel filled with rubbish, and some paltry things they called yachts to go a pleasuring upon the sea in fine weather. From hence we saw Snowdon very plain. The next flight we took was to Llanver [Llanfair] a house on the Carnarvonshire side pleasingly situated, where lives Mrs. Griffith, Wife to Mr. Griffith of Brynodol.[49] She entertained us chearfully, was sorry she was not at her other house, but insisted on our using that instead of an Inn when we went further into Llin, where no accommodation of a public kind could be hoped for. From this good lady's we rowed on to Carnarvon, where the guns were firing for the arrival of General Paoli, whom we soon saw perambulating the Town and Castle under the conduct of Sir Thomas Wynn. Paoli embraced Mr. Johnson and Sir Thomas invited us to dine with him to-morrow, then to our Inn went we, and after a bad meal set out to see the Castle. The Castle filled up all our ideas and answered all our expectations. We climbed to the top of the Eagle Tower and saw the prodigious depth below us with horror. We examined many of the recesses and saw where dungeons had been made for the confinement of criminals. The ivy here grew into absolute timber and was of such a thickness round the towers as amazed me. No ivy that I have yet seen can be compared to it. Of the Castle General Paoli said very properly that it was a fortified palace, and Mr. Johnson observed that the palace had almost wholly given way to the fortification, for we saw very few places which ever could have been state apartments. They shew one a little closet of perhaps some seven feet square, and tell one that Edward 2nd was born there, but a Lieutenant of a Man of War, who shewed us the curiosities of the place, remarked that they had no other room left entire, and therefore they called this the Prince of Wales's birth Chamber, for nothing could be more unlikely than that a Queen of England should lye in a chamber scarce capable of holding a bed. I forgot when I was in Anglesey to write down a short conversation between Mr. Johnson and his friend concerning Rowlands[50] who wrote the

Mona Antiqua and was said never to have been out of the Island. This circumstance Mr. Johnson dwelt on so long that at last the Schoolmaster said he must have been once in England however, or he could not have been ordained. Another detection of falsehood.

21st August. We had received a card last night from Colonel Wynn's lady who has apartments in one of the towers of the Castle, and this morning I breakfasted with her and went to Church. There was wonderful good singing. Mrs. Wynn's children are very fine ones, and have a strange natural genius for music; she herself sings eminently well. I returned to my nasty Inn, dressed myself and Queeney, and drove to Glynnllifore [Glynllifon][51] to dinner according to our appointment with Sir Thomas. General Paoli dined there too and our society was pleasing, though the entertainment was bad. The house, however, is stately and the master has much elegance and some knowledge, both of books and life, has travelled and has read; he has not, however, shewed much skill in the choice of his Wife, who is an empty woman of quality, insolent, ignorant, and ill bred, without either beauty or fortune to atone for her faults. She set a vile dinner before us, and on such linen as shocked one; no plate, no china to be seen, nothing but what was as despicable as herself. Mr. Johnson compared her at our return to sour small beer; she could not have been a good thing, he said, and even that poor thing was spoilt.[52] Sir Thomas shewed us his fortification on a mount which commands one of those views that the World calls romantick - rocks and sea. We returned in the evening and I put Niggey to bed, locked her door and went to supper with Mrs. Wynn at the Tower, whose sweetness and polite reception of us was a striking contrast to Lady Catherine's behaviour.

22nd August. We set forward to Brynodol,[53] where we mean to avail ourselves of Mrs. Griffith's kind invitation. On our road we dined at Llanug [Clynnog Fawr], a poor cottage where corn was had for the horses but where we should have found no food for human creatures if we had not carried cold chickens and tongue with us. We then drove forward to Mrs. Griffith's where we found every thing ready for our reception, dinner, tea, and comfortable beds. This is an excellent house, of the tight warm kind, like those near London, and the furniture all clean and new. The look from the windows, however, soon reminds you of the immence distance of this from any English habitation. The mountains rising on your right hand fatigue the eye with looking upward, and the sea, stretched out before you, tire it equally with looking forward upon total vacuity. Woods, however, of Mr. Griffith's planting shelter the left side, and the garden

Part of Fort Williamsburg and the Magazine at Glynllifon.

relieves your imagination from the terrors which such a prospect as this naturally forces on the mind. This is indeed a retreat from the World which seems wholly excluded, and in effect it is so, by mountains and by seas. The distance one is at from all relief if an accident should happen fills one with apprehension, and when I have surveyed the place of my nativity, I shall be glad to return to a land fuller of inhabitants.

23rd August. My Master took me to Bodville [Bodfel][54] where I saw the place which I first saw, and looked at the old pond with pleasure, though it is now dry. The walk of Sycamores is all cut away. I picked up an old woman who was at my christening, and she told me many things of my poor dear Mother, what she suffered at my birth and with what anxious tenderness she watched my infancy. Everything here is to me as a monument of her virtue and her sufferings, and every rough road I feel reminds me of the pain with which she passed these mountains, which I am now crossing for pleasure. The old woman, Mrs. Edwards, spoke with horror of my Father's harshness in hurrying her out so soon after so dangerous a lying-in. The present possessors of the house were very civil, and indulged all my silly curiosity, letting me look into all their hiding-places. I saw and remembered them all. From here we wished to go to Tynewydd, where my poor old friend Dick Lloyd[55] lived, who had played many a game of romps with me, and at draughts with my Father before I was seven years old. I did not remember the road to his house, though I used to go there often and beg milk, but then I walked, and now, as Mr. Johnson hates walking, and no carriage way could be found,we borrowed horses of the people at Bodvel and rode over to Tynewydd. There we found Poor Mr. Lloyd's mistress or maid, to whom he left his little all, and she shewed us where he had hung Queeney's print in the place of honour. Poor thing! he loved whatever belonged to me. I wished he had lived but to this day, how happy it would have made him. We rode on then to my Parish Church at Llanere [Llannor], which is truly wretched, and so are its few inhabitants. We examined the register and found that I was baptized on the 10th of Feburary, 1742.[56] Here I was acknowledged by a poor woman who had lived dairymaid at our house. Very fortunately I recollected some anecdotes which convinced her that I knew her, which she could scarcely believe. I gave her some little money and Mr. Thrale left a guinea to be distributed among the poor, besides five shillings for ale to drink my health forsooth. This was both prettily and kindly done, yet it neither touched nor

Bodfel Hall, Llannor.

The Parish Church, Llannor.

obliged me so much as what he said to me at Tynewydd. I was wishing Dick Lloyd alive. What signifies wishing, said Mr. Thrale, if we must wish let it be for our poor Mother who, but for that last cursed illness would have been as able to have taken this journey as yourself. This I could hardly bear to hear, or to write. It is too tender. We went to the little town of Pwllhely [Pwllheli], where Mr. Johnson would buy something, he said, in memory of his little Mistresses' Market Town; he is on every occasion so very kind, feels friendship so acutely and expresses it so delicately that it is wonderfully flattering to me to have his company. He could kind nothing to purchase but a Primmer.* Pwllhely is a piteous place to be sure, but I have a notion it is improved since the time we lived here. A coach scarce seemed a rarety now, and I have heard my Mother say that in the year 1744 all the country flocked thither to see a Sign.[57] Here Mr. Griffith, my landlord and tenant, overtook us, and brought us back to supper, and pressed us to stay tomorrow. We had an excellent supper and a hearty welcome.

24th August. Today we drove to see the Churches of which I have the impropriation. They shock me with their poverty and misery. I never imagined to myself anything half so bad. I do not know what to do for them, they are worse than one can easily conceive. We went on to Kefnamwylloch

* A primer or prayer-book.

[Cefnamwlch] and saw a man, in my mind, very respectable; he found the place a ruin, and it is now a very habitable house; he found the demesne a waste; he has divided it into fields and gardens, and has a hot-house and vinery. He gave us the first melon we have seen since we came from home. This is the Squire of Kefnamylloch, and he has possessed the estate but a year. The evening was spent in talk about business, when it was settled that we were not disposed to let a lease of our Tythes, but if we ever did entertain such an intention, Mr. Gryffith, of Brynodol, should have the preference.

25th August. This morning we took leave of our kind host, who desired we would permit him to recommend a curate in case of Jack Roberts's promotion, to which request we readily consented. I cannot here forbear to recite a ridiculous incident. When we came first to Brynodol, Mr. Griffith not being at home, we talked to his housekeeper, and among other questions Mr. Thrale asked her who was the Parson of the Parish, and where he lived. What! says she, do you mean Jack Roberts? You are come at a bad time to see Jack Roberts, for he has just got a black eye fighting for a girl with an excise man. We dined at that nasty Llanug again, which stunk so I could not bear it, so sate in the coach while they eat the meat Mr. Griffith had sent with us, for none should we have found there. The afternoon we spent with our amiable friend Mrs. Wynn, who had invited Mr. Roberts the Vicar[58] to meet us, and proposed a party of pleasure for to-morrow.

26th August. This morning we set out for the Lake of Llynnberris [Llyn Peris] at the foot of Snowdon; Mrs. Wynn accompanied us and provided a horse for me. Mr. Roberts's poney carried my Nig, and Mr. Troughton was our Captain-General. It is the wildest, stoniest, rockiest road I ever yet went, and in fifteen miles' riding we came to a cottage by the side of the lake, where we found a Harper, and Mrs. Wynn sang Welch songs to his accompaniment. Then we rowed upon the water, examined an old Castle on its borders, and saw Snowdon tower over the neighbouring hills with all the dignity of barren magnitude. Mr. Roberts had provided us a dinner at the other end of the lake, and we were entertained during our little voyage with blasts from the Copper Mills upon the mountain that made an echo of many reverberations. Goats frisking on the hills and a cataract playing at a small distance so finished the scene, that nothing, I think, could be wished for. We returned, however, somewhat too late, as we had a difficult road home and troublesome horses, but no accident happened and we spent the remainder of the evening with the Vicar, who seemed very happy to have pleased us.

27th August. We set out late as we meant only to go to Bangor, so breakfasted with Mrs. Wynn and took a kind leave of Caernarvon, where I think we have spent some pleasing and some profitable hours. Mr. Johnson says he would not have the images he has gained since he left the vale erased for £100. Mr. Roberts the Registrar received us kindly, and we slept in the soft beds which had once before been our comfort.

28th August. We went to the Cathedral and saw the Library, which is not so mean a one as I expected to find. The day and the night were spent with our friend Roberts and his Wife.

29th August. We pushed forward for Gwanynnog, and got there in the close of the evening and were very kindly received. Mr. Myddleton is apparently pleased with Mr. Thrale's company, and proud of Mr. Johnson's. The lady too is agreeable enough. The weather is very dismal.

30th August. This day was spent with Mr. Myddleton and his friends, and this seems to be the only place where we have been received and treated with attention for our own value. At other places we have been taken in because it was fit to take us, and treated according to rank, because it was right we should be so treated. Here we are loved, esteemed, and honoured, and here I daresay we might spend the whole Winter if we would.

31st August. I received letters from London, all with good accounts, except that Harry made himself sick with cherries, but that was a long while ago.

1st September. I drove down to Llewenny to see the children, and at my return wrote Mrs. Cotton word how well they were. They are really very amiable infants, and I love them next to my own.

2nd September. Queeney's Worms bite again. I gave her a quarter of a Scot's Pill last night, but it was not enough; her head does not ache, however. Mr. Thrale persecutes Bridge every day for this odious account, but cannot get it, so here we may stay for ever, I think; 'tis well we are so welcome.

Journal of a Tour in Wales with Dr. Johnson 119

Mr John Myddleton of Gwaynynog.

3rd September. We had company to dinner, but I do not recollect any particulars of the conversation or friends. I rode over to Bachygraig and saw the Estate that Sir Thomas lost for pure indolence. It is a very pretty one, and close to the house. Mr. Thrale talks of buying it again, but I think that is too kind to be true. I saw Mr. Bridge, but could not bear to talk to him; besides all talk would have been useless. I do not wish to reproach the man, and I can hardly talk temperately to one by whom I have suffered so much. I took my last look of the poor old house which has been so rever'd by some of its possessors, so mangled by the last. I shall probably see it no more.

4th September. We dined with the Rector, our kind Host's Brother.[59] He entertained us with an excellent dinner, and a thousand apologies for its being no better.

[Mrs. Thrale realised on 17th September that she had made a mistake in the dates in her Journal for the first part of September. I have therefore reconciled Mrs. Thrale's dates with those given by Johnson.]

5th September. Mr. Ellise, my tenant, came over to speak with Mr. Thrale. I charged him to pay no money without an order from Mr. Thrale, and told him that it was my desire that none of the tenants should pay their rents to Bridge in future, but to Mr. Cotton or his Agent, who has undertaken to receive them. He said that I must give him a written order. I did so in a letter to Mr. Cotton, which I signed and begged Mr. Thrale to sign too, but could not contain his compliance by any degree of earnestness though I know he approved of it too, but shewing the farmer that he did not value his Wife's request, was a better thing than securing his rents. So things stand as they did for aught I see.

[6th September.] At 12 o'clock we quitted Gwaynynog and set out in search of fresh adventures; though it was but 20 miles to Wrexham, we had much ado to get hither by nine o'clock at night; however, we came safe to our Inn. On the way we called upon Lloyd of Maesmynnan and did as we sat in the coach all the business we came into this Country to do, ordered a Letter of Attorney for Cotton and his Agent, to receive my rents, etc., and so this affair is finished.

[7th] September. From Wrexham we went on the [7th] to Chirk Castle, but I must observe that Wrexham afforded us the best lodging we have had at any Inn since we set out. Chirk Castle is by far the most enviable dwelling I have yet ever seen, ancient and spacious, full of splendour and dignity, yet with every possible convenience for obscurity and retirement. Here we saw the best Library we have been shewn in Wales, and a ridiculous Chaplain whose conversation with Mr. Johnson made me ready to burst with laughing, though I was as sick as possible, but so I am every day and all day long.

[8th] September. We rose early and went on horseback to see a prospect which greatly surpassed my expectations. It was very extensive and presented to the eye the great towns of Shrewsbury and Chester, the rocks of Merionithshire [Merionethshire], the mountain of Snowdon, the rich and fertile Counties of Worcester, Gloucester, and Hereford, with the sea on the west of Lancashire. I have never seen so noble a view for dignity, extent, and variety of objects. This night we slept at Dr. Worthington's, where the warmth of our welcome made some amends for the wretchedness of our accommodation.[60]

[9th] September. In the morning of the [9th] we saw the famous cascade at

Pistilleh Rhaiadr [Pistyll Rhaeadr], where we went and [on?] borrowed horses, and were not disappointed in our entertainment. It is a glorious waterfall. We returned to the Dr.'s, who would have detained us, but we pressed forward and arrived not late at Shrewsbury.

[10th] September. Mr. Johnson sent for Gwynn the Architect to go with us from place to place; we walked till we were weary, and Mr. Johnson snubbed the poor fellow so hard that I half pitied him, though he was so coarse a creature.

[11th] September. On the [11th] he brought a lady to wait on me to Church. We went to Church and we walked about, and we did our best, but the day went off very heavily indeed.

[12th] September. We left Shrewsbury and set forward to Lord Sandys, where, however, we could not arrive for our tackle broke and our horses tired, and we sought shelter at a little Inn five miles short of our destination. Here, however, we were more pleasantly accommodated than at any of the larger towns, and here we staid till noon the next day, before we thought of going forward. This [12th] September has been very uncomfortable. We breakfasted with Dr. Adams, a Clergyman of Shrewsbury, whose welcome, and whose breakfast, and whose conversation were so cold that I was most impatient of delay. When we got further it rained pitiably, and we walked up a steep hill they called Wenlock Edge till our feet were very wet and dirty. The evening made matters worse, but the little Inn at Hartlebury, where all was better than expectation, comforted and refreshed us. Queeney has caught cold again.

[13th] September. We came to Lord Sandys who received us with all possible kindness and entertained us with a liberality of friendship which cannot be surpassed. The Lady's attention to her friends makes more than amends for her ignorance and deformity. I liked her the first day and loved her the last.

[14th] September. These good creatures carried us to Worcester, where we saw the Cathedral, which is a very fine one. The china manufactory we likewise examined, and I bought a bottle and basin to give away. I was very ill[61] in the evening, when Lady Sandys's care of me was tender and not teazing.

[15th] September. I staid within and was careful of myself and my child. The evening was spent among books and literary talk, and Mr. Johnson was sorry we were going away. We lived here very comfortably.

[16th] September. We dressed and dined at Hagley, where the day passed in the common formalities till the evening came and the ladies pressed me to play at cards, notwithstanding all my excuses, with an ill-bred but irresistible importunity. I played to please them and I think won three shillings, which they paid for the pleasure of enjoying my inferiority in the only science wherein I could be found inferior to them. Mr. Johnson sate to read awhile and then walked about, when Mr. Lyttelton advertised if he did not use his candle to put it out.[62]

[17th September.] I have made some mistake in the dates for here is the 17th on Saturday. It is Hetty's birthday, and she spent the most part of it in Hagley Park, which is indeed the beautiful spot it has been called. The house is spacious enough, well-decorated with pictures, and eminent for its commodiousness and disposition of the rooms. One sees no offices of any sort, which, as Mr. Thrale made me observe, is an elegance peculiar to this place, and he says true, I have seen it nowhere else. The dedication of particular seats to particular friends who were fond of them, has something pleasing and tender in it, but the other inscriptions are idle and useless, and give more plague than pleasure. Such was the morning. The evening dragg'd somewhat heavy. Cards again and cruel vexation to me, but to-night I scarce troubled myself to hold them. The ladies had made themselves so disagreeable to me that I thought they deserved no unpleasant compliance from me, and they shall have none.

18th September was Sunday and we went to church. It is a very pretty one, and the family monuments are full of taste and elegance. The late Lord,[63] it seems, had brought his Lucy's Corpse from some other consecrated ground when his death approached and desired she might be put in the same herse and the same grave with him. When one hears of such tenderness one is inclined to think that he who has never loved never was happy. His finest feelings lay by till they rusted. On this day Sir Edwd and Lady Littleton, Lord Dudley, and Miss Ward dined with us. Sir Edward Littleton seems to be a very agreeable man. The afternoon pass'd well enough with the help of the company, and on the 19th we came away.

[19th September.] The weather was most exceedingly cold and rainy, yet we resolved not to pass the Leasowes without taking a look. I shut Queeney safe, however, and looked over Mr. Shenstone's woods and walks with more pleasure than I thought one could have obtained upon such a displeasing day. The cascades, however, are so lovely, so unartificial to appearance, and so frequent that one must be delighted, and confess that if one had to chuse among all the places one has seen the Leasowes should be the choice to inhabit oneself, while Keddlestone or Hagley should be reserved for the gardener to show on a Sunday to travelling fools and starers. While Mr. Thrale and Mr. Johnson went up to have a nearer view of the waterfall, I sat by the boathouse and made the following verses:-

> To Shenstone in his Grot retired
> My truest praise I'll pay;
> And view with just contempt inspire
> The Glitter of the Gay.
>
> From Keddlestone's offensive glare
> From Chatsworth's proud cascade
> From artful Hagley I repair
> To thine and nature's shade.
>
> When Rubens thus too fiercely burns,
> When Lucan glows with rage
> The soul to softer Guido turns
> And Virgil's Pastoral Page.[64]

From this sweet seclusion, for such it appears, we travelled on to Birminghan, having on our road met Mr. Herne, the present possessor of the Leasowes, who offered us a thousand civilities and pressed us to return. We went forward, however, and got to busy Birmingham early in the afternoon. Mr. Johnson sent for his friend Hector, from whom I hoped to extract some juvenile anecdotes of Mr. Johnson, but I was by this time too sick for relation or enquiry and was forced to go to bed by 9 o'clock.

20th September. We breakfasted with Mr. Hector, who took us to Clay's new paper manufactury, where we saw many curiosities and purchased some. The hardness of the paper is really astonishing and the ware equally elegant and durable. I like it extremely. From hence we went to Bolton's. He showed us his

Buttons at 3s. the six dozen, and his watch chains at two pence each, we saw the whole process of the manufacture, and found Mr. Bolton a very intelligent man. When evening came we dined and talked. Mr. Johnson said how much he had been in love with Mr. Hector's sister,[65] the old lady who made breakfast for us in the morning, and when I recollected her figure I thought she had the remains of a beauty. I was sick again and obliged to retire very early. I was used on these occasions to be sick only in the morning, but now I am scarce ever otherwise.

21 September. We rose early as we had fifty miles and more to Woodstock, where we proposed Inning, but these miles are very different from those between Shrewsbury and Worcester, when our horses tired, our tackle broke, our roads were deep and our hills high. We had on this day nothing to retard us, and at the last stage of the journey Mr. Seward[66] came up to the coach-side and so went with us to Woodstock, where we sent for our friend Mr. King and consulted how to see Blenheim in the morning.

[22nd September.] Horses were accordingly provided and we rode about the Park. I had a lame steed at first, but when the rain drove Queeney into the Coach I mounted her little Pad, as King called him, and galloped about with great delight. This park and house so swallows up everything that one had seen before, that for the moment everything is forgotten. Here is the finest piece of made water in the world, I believe. A lake of three hundred acres. Among the pictures none pleased me more than a fine Claude, one of the finest indeed I ever saw. There is a Head of Dorothea by Raphael highly estimated, and a Vandyke or two, which I prize above the Rubenses, given to the Duke by some foreign state, I forget what. Lord Blandford[67] begged to see me, but I declined the honour as he had the Hooping Cough. I hear the Duke and Duchess were very attentive and polite, and said they would have asked us to dinner but that they were engaged abroad. We went late to Oxford, where we got better accommodations than I hoped for.

23rd September. We saw some of the wonders of Oxford; the only things new to me were General Gaise's [Guise's] collection of pictures,[68] among which I prefer Murillo's two boys, Titian's Mistress, Guido's St. John, a dying Magdalen by Domenichino and Susanna by Carracci.

24th September. We saw more curiosities, some books in the Bodleian[69] finely illuminated, the Pomfret Marbles, among which Tully seems the most valuable, and the Arundel Marbles,[70] where one looks with reverence upon the original Treaty of Peace after the Battle of Marathon. We dined in the Hall at University College, where I sat in the seat of honour as Locum Tenens forsooth; and saw the ceremonies of the Grace Cup[71] and Butler's Book. Mr. Coulson entertained us with liberality and with kindness; I was flattered and was pleased and was not sick at night, but made up my Journal instead of going to bed. We drank tea in the Common Room, had a World of talk, and passed the evening with cheerfulness and comfort. I like Mr. Coulson much and pressed him to come to Streatham with a very honest importunity. I shall wish to see him again.

25th September. On this day likewise we ran about the Town and saw whatever we could of Colleges, Halls, and Libraries, the Picture Gallery[72] and Museum, and dined with Vansittart, whose politeness and desire to oblige would be still more valuable than they are did one not easily observe that all is a mere effort to get rid of himself, not to oblige his friends. This unhappy man has had by accident his spirits much disordered and seeks that refuge from coxcomry and assiduity which has been denied him by literature, and that liveliness of disposition which seems natural to him.

26th September. The Printing House,[73] etc., filled up the morning, and we dined at our Inn with Seward, Coulson, Johnson, and a cousin of Mr. Seward's, a student of Oxford. The afternoon gave time for conversation and scope for argument in which poor Mr. Coulson was defeated and fretful.

27th September. We went to New Inn Hall,[74] where Mr. Thrale had lived with Chambers on the occasion of Lord North's installation. He seemed happy to see it again. In a few hours we set off for Benson with intent to see our possessions in those parts, but such was the weather all pleasure in walking or riding was hopeless. We sat at our Inn therefore and were quiet.

28th September. We drove to the farm house and saw Crowmarsh.[75] Mr. Lovegrove seemed to have everything very neat and bright about his place; his Wife I take to be a drunkard. It is a delightful Country. We went on late to Burke's.

29th September. Last night we were received with open arms by our friends at Beaconsfield; each seemed to contend who should be kindest, but to-day Mr. Burke himself was obliged to go out somewhere about Election matters. There was an old Mr. Lowndes[76] dined with us and got very drunk talking Politics with Will Burke[77] and my Master after dinner. Lord Verney[7] and Edmund came home at night very much flustered with liquor, and I thought how I had spent three months from home among dunces of all ranks and sorts, but had never seen a man drunk till I came among the Wits. This was accidental indeed, but what of that? it was so.

30th September. When I rose Mr. Thrale informed me that the Parliament was suddenly dissolved and that all the World was to bustle, that we were to go to Southwark, not to Streatham, and canvass away. I heard the first part of this report with pleasure, the latter with pain; nothing but a real misfortune could, I think, affect me so much as the thoughts of going to Town thus to settle for the Winter before I have had any enjoyment of Streatham at all, and so all my hopes of pleasure blow away. I thought to have lived at Streatham in quiet and comfort, have kissed my children and cuffed them by turns, and had a place always for them to play in, and here I must be shut up in that odious dungeon, where nobody will come near me, the children are to be sick for want of air *and I am never to see a face but Mr. Johnson's*. Oh, what a life that is! and how truly do I abhor it! At noon, however, I saw my Girls and thought Susan vastly improved. At evening I saw my Boys and liked them very well too. How much is there always to thank God for! but I dare not enjoy poor Streatham lest I should be forced to quit it.

Notes on Mrs Thrale's Journal

N.B. Mrs. Thrale and Mrs. Piozzi.

In 1781 Henry Thrale died from a stroke brought on by his gormandising. Three years later, to everyone's consternation, his widow married a gentlemanly, Catholic, Italian musician called Gabriel Piozzi; to everyone's chagrin, this ill-assorted pair lived happily ever after.

Mrs. Piozzi continued to pursue an active and stimulating career on the periphery of literature. In 1786 she published her *Anecdotes of the late Samuel Johnson*, and two years later her correspodence with him. All extracts attributed to Mrs. Piozzi in both sets of Notes are drawn from her *Anecdotes*, letters, or her miscellaneous writings known as *Thraliana*.

Mrs. Piozzi is thus young Mrs. Thrale writ large.

1. Joseph Baretti (1719-89), from Piedmont, was a miscellaneous writer, best known for his Italian/English Dictionary (1760). He became a friend of Johnson who introduced him to the Thrales with whom he lived for three years, becoming Queeney's tutor in French and Italian. He accompanied Johnson and the Thrales to France in 1775.

2. Lady Lade was Henry Thrale's sister.

3. Ralph Smith was Thrale's first cousin.

4. This was the widow of Thrale's other first cousin, Henry Smith, and her eighteen year old son, Henry.

5. As the coach travelled up Watling Street from St. Albans to Dunstable, Mrs. Thrale was reminded of long, happy months she had spent as a girl with her parents and relations at two nearby houses: East Hyde, the house of her grandmother, Lady Cotton, some two miles north of Harpenden, and Offley Place, the estate of her uncle, Sir Thomas Salusbury, which lies about eight miles north-west of Dunstable and two miles from Hitchin.

6. Mrs. Piozzi recollects: "When I went with him to Lichfield, and came downstairs to breakfast at the inn, my dress did not please him, and he made me alter it entirely before he would stir a step with us about the town, saying most satirical things concerning the appearance I made in a riding-habit." Johnson

rather wanted Mrs. Thrale to appear to advantage before his friends.

7. A Pulse glass was a glass tube with a bulb at each end, or at one end only, containing spirits of wine or rarefied air. When grasped by the hand, it showed a momentary agitation, repeated at each beat of the pulse.

8. During the Civil War, Lichfield was a Royalist stronghold. It lay on the road from the north-east of England to Oxford, along which men, arms and supplies were sent to the King's headquarters at Oxford. The city suffered three sieges between 1643 and 1646. The interior of the cathedral was vandalised by the Parliamentary forces, and later on the central spire was brought crashing down by artillery fire, destroying the chancel and the choir. After the Restoration the cathedral was rebuilt but it fell into decay during the eighteenth century and was in a sorry state at the time of Johnson's visit. "Fanatics" was a term applied to zealous Non-Conformists and hence Parliamentarians.

9. The corner house in Breadmarket Street where Johnson was born is now the Johnson Birthplace Museum. The house was built by Michael Johnson, Samuel's father, in 1707 for his business. The large room on the ground floor was his bookshop, the family lived below stairs, while the bedrooms for the family, visitors, and servants were upstairs. Samuel Johnson was born in the room over the bookshop on the first floor. The house is owned and generously maintained by the Lichfield City Council.

10. Peter Garrick was David Garrick's elder brother and very much like him in appearance [See Johnson Note 8].

11. The two Sosias were characters in a popular play by Dryden called *Amphitryon* or *The Two Sosia's* (pub. 1690). In the play Sosia is Amphitryon's slave. Jupiter, in order to seduce Amphitryon's wife, takes the form of Amphitryon and is aided and abetted by Mercury who appears as Sosia's double.

12. Arthur Chichester, Earl of Donegal. The Fisherwick estate was sold in 1804 and the house later demolished. The pillars of the façade (sold for the cost of transport) were re-erected in 1822 outside the George Hotel, Walsall.

13. Town-Malling, now known as West Malling, is some six miles WNW of Maidstone. Here lived Francis Brooke, a retired attorney and a close friend of Ralph Thrale. Johnson and the Thrales had visited him at Brooke House in Swan Street in 1768. Brooke House was destroyed by fire in 1980 but was rebuilt and

the façade restored in 1984; it now houses a branch of the National Westminster Bank. A stream, rising in St. Leonards, ran (and still runs) through this part of the village to join the Addington Brook. Originally it made its way from the Abbey grounds into the extensive garden of Brooke House, which included a canal and pleasure grounds reaching down to the London road. The canal dropped down in shallow steps to form an attractive cascade. Today the elaborate garden is no more and the stream, emerging from the walls of the Abbey grounds, is taken off under Swan Street.

14. Scots Pills, or Anderson's Scots Pills, were a popular patent medicine introduced by Dr. Patrick Anderson, a physician who practised in Edinburgh, London, and Paris in the early seventeenth century. According to his book, *Grana Angelica* (1635), he obtained the formula in Venice in 1603. The pilulae aloes et myrrhae of the British Pharmacopeia contain their essential ingredients. Advertised as being efficacious in almost every case, the pills were widely used as a purgative for three centuries and were still on sale in the early twentieth century.

15. The original Ilam Hall, the seat of the Port family, which the party visited, no longer exists, except for the stable block. The house was rebuilt between 1821 and 1826 in the Gothic style but three quarters of it was demolished before the last war. The remaining part, now owned by the National Trust, is used as an International Youth Hostel. What is left of the formal Italian gardens belongs to the early 19th c., yet it is easy to visualise how attractive the parkland and woods appeared in the late 18th c., sweeping down to the River Manifold with Hinkley Wood rising on the opposite side. Ilam has a superb situation, looking eastwards down the Manifold valley towards Thorpe Cloud and Bunster Hill, the "Portals of Dovedale", which Mrs. Thrale admired so much.

16. Matlock Dale is one of the most dramatic limestone gorges in England. The River Derwent winds southwards through the dale of Matlock Bath, which is dominated on the left by the enormous 350 ft. bulk of High Tor, with the wooded steep of the Heights of Abraham opposite it. It was the former that the party walked up.

17. Probably the eldest son (b.1748) of William Abney of Measham Hole near Ashby-de-la-Zouch.

18. Richard Arkwright, originally a barber in Bolton, a centre of the cotton

industry, invented a machine for spinning cotton. In 1771 he erected the first water-powered cotton mill at Cromford near Matlock Bath, installing machinery for manufacturing ribbed stockings and, later, calico. Further developments of his patent led to the performance in one machine of the whole process of yarn manufacture. His mill became the model for others throughout Britain and abroad and earned him the title of "Father of the Factory System". Arkwright's mill is currently being restored by the Arkwright Society and is open to visitors.

19. Hugo Meynell, of Bradley Hall near Ashbourne, was a famous sportsman and MFH. The old Hall has long been demolished and the new Hall stands opposite the church. The Meynell Kennels are also no longer in existence but cottages known as "The Kennels" stand on their site.

20. See Johnson Note 24.

21. This was Molton Walhouse of Hatherton in Staffordshire [see Johnson Note 18].

22. Cotquean = a man that acts the housewife, and meddles with women's matters. Deist = one who believes in the existence of a God but rejects revealed religion. (O.E.D.)

23. Buxton developed as a spa at the end of the 18th c. under the guidance of the 5th Duke of Devonshire. In 1774, however, it was, architecturally, in its infancy; John Carr had yet to build the superb Crescent and the Riding School and Stables.

24. This is a reference to the custom of 'Blessing the Brine' on Ascension Day. On that day the 'Old Biot', as the original brine pit or salt spring was called, was dressed with green boughs, flowers, and ribbons. The inhabitants assembled in gala dress around it and sang a hymn of thanksgiving for this natural blessing. They then passed the rest of the day in dancing, feasting and merry-making. With the decline in the trade, the custom appears to have been discontinued about 1750.

25. Johnson later wrote to Mrs. Thrale on 13 Nov. 1783: "Do you not remember how he rejoiced in having *no* park; He could not disoblige his neighbours by sending them *no* venison."

26. This was Corbet D'Avenant, later Sir Corbet Corbet, from nearby Adderley

Hall in Shropshire who married Hester ('Hetty') Salusbury Cotton. Adderley Hall was demolished some years ago, but there is a monument to the happy couple in the south transept of the original part of St. Peter's Church, Adderley, which was vested in the Redundant Churches Fund in 1977.

27. Mrs. Piozzi wrote later:
"I have seldom seen him much more angry than he was with me, one morning, at West Chester; while some gentleman of the town was shewing us the curiosities of so ancient and respectable a place:– for our Doctor was slow, and heavy, and short-sighted; and by the time he had begun to examine and discuss one thing, our brisker Cicerone set us all going in chace of another. This went on a while; and I saw impatience struggling with civility in Johnson's countenance, when he suddenly asked me – in order to stop him, I suppose – "Pray what is this gentleman's name, who accompanies us so officiously?" – "I think they call him *Harold* (replied I); and perhaps you'll find him to be of the family of *Harold Harefoot,* he runs with us at such a rate."

28. This tapestry, once bright with glowing colours,depicts the confrontation between St. Paul and Elymas,the Cyprus sorcerer, before the Roman Governor (Acts 13.11). Some eleven feet high and fifteen feet wide, it was woven at Mortlake from a copy of one of Raphael cartoons for the Sistine Chapel, and was eventually presented to the Cathedral about 1660. It hung behind the High Altar until 1843 when it was removed to the north transept to make way for a mosaic of the Last Supper. When new organ pipes needed to be installed in the transept, the tapestry was again moved, this time to the Refectory, where it hangs today, faded and unregarded, above the servery.

29. The memorial by Michael Rysbrack (1683-1770) stands at the west end of this attractive church. Wynne had it erected several years before his death and composed the inscription himself. The date of his death was left blank to be filled in later. The inscription reads as follows:-
"William Wynne of Tower D.D. sometime Fellow of All Souls College in Oxford and Rector of Llanvechen in this Diocese departed this life 3rd March 1776 Aged 77. In conformity to ancient usage, from a proper regard to decency, and a concern for the health of his Fellow Creatures, he was mov'd to give particular directions for being buried in the adjoining Church-yard, and not in the Church.

And as he scorn'd flattering of others while living, he has took care to prevent being flatter'd himself, when dead, by causing this small memorial to be set up in his life time – God be merciful to me a sinner."

30. Mrs. Thrale is perhaps being a little uncharitable. Mrs. Shipley was formerly Anna Maria Mordaunt, the niece of an earl, and one of Queen Caroline's maids-of-honour.

31. This valley tradition is the 'plygain', a carol service held in the parish church between 3 a.m. and 6 a.m. on Christmas morning. It developed from the midnight mass of the pre-Reformation period and became an important part of the nativity celebrations. Churches were decorated with candles; their light was thought to have a symbolic significance. The plygain began with a shortened version of the morning prayer and was followed by carols, religious and doctrinal in content, sung to the popular ballad tunes of the day. This type of celebration nearly died out, but there has been a revival of interest recently and plygain services have been held in the evenings between mid-December and mid-January, particularly in Montgomeryshire. Hundreds of plygain carols have survived and a selection, with their texts, can be found in a series of recordings, *Welsh Folk heritage* (1977).

32. In a letter to Queeney in September 1803, Mrs. Piozzi wrote of the church in which her father was buried, "It was a Place like a stable you know; and we have made a Vault for ourselves and my poor Ancestors, whose bones we found by digging under the Altar." Yet the church of Corpus Christi at Tremeirchion, attractive and well-kept as it is, is something of a disappointment for those seeking evidence of Mrs. Thrale and her second husband. The vault in which they were buried, then outside the church, is now covered by the north transept. There is simply a tablet inside the chapel, which records:

> Near this place are interred the remains of
> HESTER LYNCH PIOZZI
> 'Doctor Johnson's Mrs. Thrale.'
> Born 1741. Died 1821.
> Witty, vivacious and charming, in an age of genius:
> She ever held a foremost place.

And this tablet was only erected through the efforts of Mr. O. Butler Fellowes as part of the tributes to Johnson on the two hundredth anniversary of his birth. There is no reference anywhere to Piozzi – which is rather hard considering he paid for extensive repairs to the church while they were living nearby at Brynbella.

33. This was the Chapel of Lleweni. [See Johnson Note 58]

34. Thoyt's Copper Mill was one of several mills established in the valley of the River Wandle by the mid-18th century. William Thoyt's mill was built within the boundary walls of Merton Abbey by what is now High Street, Merton. Today its site is overwhelmed by a giant Savacentre. Thoyt's mill produced various domestic utensils as well as copper plates for calico printing.

35. In Greek mythology Danae was shut up in a tower by her father, Acrisius, because an oracle prophesied that he would be killed by his daughter's son. However, Zeus, who loved Danae, visited her in a shower of gold and she bore a son, Perseus, who many years later accidentally fulfilled the prophecy.

Andromeda, chained to a rock as a sacrifice to a sea-monster, was found, rescued, and married by Perseus.

Alcyone was the wife of Ceyx who was drowned at sea. Moved by her despair, the Gods re-united them by changing them into birds; she became a kingfisher (halcyon) and he became a tern.

36. Bodryddan Hall, the home of William Shipley, Dean of St. Asaph (1774-1826) and son of the Bishop there, who had married Penelope Yonge, the heiress of Bodryddan. It had previously been the home of the Stapleton family and Mrs. Frances Cotton (née Stapleton) had spent her childhood there. Today the house, considerably altered since Johnson's visit, belongs to Lord Lansdowne of the Rowley-Conwy family and is open to the public between June and September.

The Memorial Plaque in Tremeirchion Church.

In the Big Dining Room are portraits of the Bishop of St. Asaph (by Reynolds) and of his wife, Mrs. Shipley, (by Hogarth) and of their son, the Dean. The Dean, as evinced by his picture, was a man of powerful personality and forceful views, and his long reign is commemorated by a statue in a corner of the west end of the cathedral.

37. Mrs. Piozzi in a letter to Duppa commented:
"Dr Johnson loved a *fine* dinner, but eat perhaps more heartily of a *coarse* one – boiled beef or veal pie; fish he seldom passed over though he said that he only valued the sauce, and that every body eat the first as a vehicle for the second. When he poured oyster sauce over plum pudding, and the melted butter flowing from the toast into his chocolate, one might surely say that he was nothing less than delicate." Again, in her *Anecdotes*, she writes that "a leg of pork boiled till it dropped from the bone, a veal-pye with plums and sugar, or the outside cut of a salt buttock of beef, were his favourite dainties."

Of one occasion during their stay at Lleweni, Mrs. Thrale wrote:
"When we went into Wales together, and spent some time at Mr. Cotton's at Lleweni, one day at dinner I meant to please Mr. Johnson particularly, with a dish of very young peas. 'Are they not charming?' said I to him, while he was eating them. 'Perhaps they would be so – to a pig.' This is given only as an instance of the peculiarity of his manner, and which had in it no intention to offend."

38. tr. If only they knew how lucky they were. (Virgil).

39. Mr. & Mrs. D'Avenant were staying at Lleweni, too. They had caused great consternation at Combermere on 24th July.

40. Edward Bridge had acted as Agent for the Bachygraig estate for many years. Bridge lived in the tiny hamlet of Bodfari near the forge. In his business correspondence, which is held by the John Rylands University Library in Manchester, he is constantly apologising for delays in the transaction of business, usually blaming this on his poor state of health (rheumatism, gout, gravel, etc.) and, Cassandra-like, presaging woe at every turn. One story, however, relieves the gloom. In the autumn of 1761, Sir Thomas Salusbury sent him up a ploughman, Thomas Green, plus ploughboy and a team of four horses from his estate at Offley to sow wheat at Bachygraig. Green proved to be a difficult and rather expensive visitor for he was apparently accustomed to a diet far superior to that of "our top farmers". Bridge commented: "I am surprised that

Hetfordshire men have so bad an idea of Wales. I suppose that they think that there's nothing but rock and stones to eat in this country, and if so he must be a bold resolute fellow who ventures amongst us without a set of good teeth." The year before the Thrales' visit, Bridge was in serious financial trouble, was arrested for debt and narrowly escaped prosecution. Against this background Mr. & Mrs. Thrale met Bridge on several occasions to discuss the problems of her Welsh estate but the outcome was most unsatisfactory. Mrs. Thrale's mother, who knew Bridge of old, thought him "the worthiest of Mankind [but he has] plundered us for 20 Years most grossly." As we shall see, matters came to a head on their return from the Lleyn Peninsula. Thrale compelled Bridge to produce certain estate accounts, by which time Mrs. Thrale could no longer bring herself to talk to him. Bridge was summarily dismissed by Thrale and it was arranged that Mrs. Thrale's rents should be collected by her cousin and his agent in future.

41. Poor Queeney suffered from worms during the tour. Her mother was still dosing her for this complaint over a year later when they were travelling in France. Mrs. Thrale was well-known in her circle for her passion for doctoring her children; she was always ready to prescribe and administer pills, purges, and cold plunges for a variety of conditions.

42. Mrs. Parry was the wife of Richard Parry of Llanrhaiadr Hall, a property which had once, in fact, belonged to the Salusburys. The handsome hall is now cut off by a bypass from the village, with its attractive church and almshouses, and is a private nursing home.

43. Mrs. Bunbury, formerly Catherine Horneck, married Henry Bunbury (1750-1811) in 1771. The lively and amusing Bunbury was an amateur artist and caricaturist and the friend of Goldsmith (as was his bride), Garrick and Reynolds. Besides painting the young Mrs. Bunbury's portrait, Reynolds had also painted Bunbury as a youth and later was to paint their young son.

44. The County of Caernarfonshire included the Lleyn Peninsula which juts out into the Irish Sea and forms the northern arm of Cardigan Bay.

45. Oliver Goldsmith, dramatist and poet, had died in poverty on 4th April, aged only 44. He had been a member, and a welcome one, of the Johnson circle for some years. Despite Goldsmith's social shortcomings, which led Horace Walpole to call him an "inspired idiot" and Garrick to describe him as one:

... for shortness called Noll.
Who wrote like an angel, and talk'd like poor Poll,

Johnson respected him and much admired his work. At his death Johnson wrote: "He had raised money and squandered it, by every artifice of acquisition and folly of expence. But let not his frailties be remembered; he was a very great man."

46. With some reason. Before Lucy's death the previous year, Mrs. Thrale had already lost three other daughters, two through what was almost certainly meningitis – a sad comment on the infant mortality rate of the time.

47. The Cathedral of St. Deiniol at Bangor is about the same size as many of the larger English parish churches and contains relatively little of remark. The Library was orginally built early in the 18th c. over the mediaeval chapter room and vestry. However, two years after Mrs. Thrale's visit, this upper storey was redesigned and rebuilt. Some years ago all the books, including the famous Bishop Anian's *Pontifical*, were transferred to the University College of North Wales across the road. Thus no trace of the library remains today and that part of the upper floor is used as a choir vestry.

48. His grandson was the famous Marquess of Anglesey, commander of the cavalry at Waterloo and second-in-command to the Duke of Wellington. Plas Newydd, still the family home and now open to the public, contains a splendid mural in the saloon by Rex Whistler. It also houses an exhibition of this artist's work and a small cavalry museum. Originally built in the 16th century for the Griffith family, the house was altered and enlarged in the 1750s for Sir Nicholas Bayly. It is this structure that Johnson and Mrs Thrale saw. A few years later, between 1783 and 1799, the house assumed its present late Georgian Gothic form. The attractive, castellated stable block was added in 1797. The Chapel referred to later in the entry for 20th August was converted during the 1930s into a dining-room with bedrooms and bathrooms on the floor above.

49. Mary, daughter and heiress of William Wynn of Llanfair Hall, married Hugh Griffith, who was Sheriff of Caernarfonshire in 1777/78. Llanfair Hall is an Italianate-style house on rising ground commanding extensive views of the Menai Strait. It is still in private hands and is virtually unchanged.

50. Henry Rowlands (1655-1723) was a Welsh cleric and influential antiquary. His most important work was *Mona Antiqua Restaurata*, published in 1723, a survey of the ancient remains of Anglesey.

51. Glynllifon Park was a red-brick mansion built by Sir Thomas Wynn in 1751 but unfortunately destroyed by fire in 1836. The present splendid classical house and stables were built by the 3rd Lord Newborough in 1837-46 and the wing added by his successor between 1889 and 1893. The mansion and estate is now owned by the Gwynedd County Council and houses the Glynllifon College. The park is open to visitors.

Fort Williamsburg stands on a hill inside the park. It was built by Sir Thomas in 1761 and extended between 1773 and 1776 during a period of fear of a French invasion. It consists of a large area enclosed by a dry walled moat. Inside, a narrow tunnel leads to a knoll, surrounded by a deep ditch, on which stands a tower with the inscription 'Williamsbourg Fort' over the door. Outside is a small look-out platform built over a magazine. Sadly the tower is disused and decrepit but it commands fine views of cliffs and coast to the west. In 1762 Sir Thomas raised 'The Carnarvonshire Militia' to protect his estate and in 1775 he started building another, and much more effective fort (Fort Belan) at the entrance to the Menai Strait.

52. Mrs. Piozzi recalled Johnson's reaction:

"'That woman', cried Mr. Johnson, 'is like sour small beer, the beverage of her table and produce of the wretched country she lives in. Like that she could never have been a good thing, and even that bad thing is spoiled.'"

53. Pennant describes Brynodol as "being situated on the side of a hill, commanding a vast view of a flat, woodless tract, the sea and a noble mass of mountains." It was built in the mid-18th century (Johnson describes it as "new built") and is virtually unchanged.

54. Bodfel Hall is a three-storied, seventeenth century house, originally planned as a gatehouse, with its doorway flanked by Doric columns (decayed). By the middle of the 18th century it had been converted into a dwelling house with the gate-passage being blocked by an added stair. There is no trace of any building to which the gatehouse would have given access. Here Mrs. Thrale was born on 16th January 1741.

Today the Hall is occupied by a Mrs. Morris and her two sons who have developed a craft centre, caravan park and a children's playground in the grounds. Although the Hall appears uncared for, the attractive pond (it is a large pond) is now full with an islet in the middle. Many years later Mrs. Piozzi wrote the following poem:

Lines on Bodfel Hall, the Birthplace of Mrs. H. L. Piozzi.

... 2. Nor ye, who, vers'd in critic lore,
O'er Johnson's *Lives* incessant pore,
And know how, propp'd with care, the sage
Prolonged his course another stage,
Forget – as every page you turn,
With profit, or with rapture burn, –
To Bodfel ye the pleasure owe.

3. And ye, who, how with fluent tongue,
As oft he spoke his friends among,
Read – that, with wit and wisdom fraught,
Some he rebuk'd, and some he taught;
Learn, as the tales before your eyes,
Fix'd in immortal page still rise, –
To Bodfel ye the pleasure owe.

6. To Bodfel, then, a grateful song
Its woods and meads and streams along,
Thy aid I supplicate, O Muse,
Nor thou the supplicated boon refuse;
So may I haply forth to fame
The short, but gracious, tale proclaim; –
To Bodfel I these pleasures owe.

55. Richard Lloyd (d.1771) was a boon companion of John Salusbury, Mrs. Thrale's father, when he and his family lived at Bodfel Hall. He acted for many years as his agent in connection with the tithes of Tydweiliog and Llangwnnadl. He lived at Tynewydd, a substantial late seventeenth century farmhouse with an eighteenth century wing. Although only a mile from Bodfel Hall as the crow flies, Ty Newydd is not easy to find and is best approached by the narrow, uphill road running north from Llannor. It is occupied today by William Lloyd-Jones, a descendant. There is a grave slab to Richard Lloyd in Llannor churchyard.

56. Mrs. Thrale was baptised at the thirteenth century church of the Holy Cross at Llannor on 10th February 1741 – not 1742 as she imperfectly recollects.

57. I have been unable to trace this reference with any certainty. In the 1740s evangelical 'exhorters', spearheaded by Howel Harris. [See Johnson Note 103] were spreading the Methodist message and establishing Societies throughout the Lleyn Peninsula. Pwllheli was regarded as the mother church of the tiny

Dissenting groups in the area. There is, perhaps, a connection with the local tradition that the terror caused by a partial eclipse of the sun (as in film dramas involving African natives) was utilised by the fiery Methodist preachers for their own ends.

58. This was Mr. Roberts, the Vicar of St. Mary's.

59. See Johnson Note 108.

60. Mrs Thrale and her companions almost certainly rode out to the top of Wern Tower, a prominent local hill a mile and a half to the north-west of the castle. While staying at Douai during her visit to France in 1775, Mrs. Thrale wrote in her journal for 6th November: "The Chamber I sleep in is a spacious one and was sweet enough when I chose it, but such a stink was got into it at night as I never smelt a worse but at Llanrhaiadr."

61. Mrs. Thrale was once again in the throes of morning sickness. Soon after she returned to London, Mrs. Thrale fell from her horse and Johnson reported that she "cut her face and bruised her body, but she has not miscarried, and will soon be well." Mrs. Thrale gave birth to a girl, Frances Ann, on 4 May 1775 but, sadly, the sickly child died before Christmas.

62. Mrs. Piozzi later wrote: "Mrs. Lyttleton, ci-devant Caroline Bristow, forced me to play at whist against my liking, and her husband took away Johnson's candle that he wanted to read by at the other end of the room."

63. George, Lord Lyttelton (1709-73), often referred to as the "Good Lord Lyttelton." His first wife, Lucy Fortescue, died in January 1747 aged twenty-nine and had been buried at Over Arley in Staffordshire. [See Johnson Note 126]

64. Peter Paul Rubens (1577-1640), greatest of the Flemish painters.

Marcus Annaeus Lucanus (AD 39-65), a brilliant young poet who conspired unsuccessfully against Nero (another poet!) and was commanded to take his own life. His one surviving poem is the *Pharsalia*, the finest Latin epic after the *Aeneid*.

Guido Reni (1575-1642), a much-admired follower of Raphael.
Publius Vergilius Maro (70-19 BC), author of the *Aeneid* and of charming pastoral poems contained in the *Georgics* and the *Eclogues*.

65. This was Hector's sister, Mrs. Carless, a clergyman's widow. When Johnson and Boswell visited the house again in March 1776, Johnson declared: "She was the first woman with whom I was in love. It dropt out of my head imperceptibly; but she and I shall always have a kindness for each other." Boswell continues: "On our return from Mr. Bolton's, Mr. Hector took me to his house, where we found Johnson sitting placidly at tea, with his first love; who though now advanced in years, was a genteel woman, very agreeable, and well-bred."

66. William Seward was a particular friend of the Thrales.

67. George Spencer Churchill, afterwards 5th Duke of Marlborough, born 1766. He was the eldest son of the Duke of Marlborough. In 1762 the latter married Caroline, only daughter of John, fourth Duke of Bedford, a most accomplished woman, who made Blenheim the seat of a very fashionable and exclusive coterie. Her musical parties and private theatricals were famous.

68. Mrs. Thrale visited Christ Church. General John Guise, formerly an undergraduate at Christ Church, had a long and distinguished military career. In 1765 he died and bequeathed his collection of pictures, which he greatly valued, to his old college. Walpole records that the college arranged for the pictures to be repaired but that the restorer unfortunately repainted and utterly spoiled them all.

69. The Bodleian Library was restored and developed by Sir Thomas Bodley and opened in 1602. Until the founding of the British Museum in 1753 it was the chief library in England. It was housed in rooms over the Divinity School when Mrs. Thrale was shown some of its treasures.

70. Mrs. Thrale saw this collection of Greek and Roman sculpture in the Old Ashmolean Museum in Broad Street, built in 1678-1683 for Elias Ashmole's collection of curiosities. Today the sculpture is displayed in the Randolph Gallery in the new Ashmolean Museum (completed 1848) in Beaumont Street. The Arundel Marbles were bought in 1624 at Smyrna and elsewhere for Thomas Howard (1586-1646), Earl of Arundel. The inscriptions were presented to the University by his grandson, Lord Henry Howard, in 1667. In 1775, Henrietta Louisa, Dowager Countess of Pomfret, gave the sculpture from the Arundel collection to the museum.

71. The ceremony of the Grace Cup, or Loving Cup as it is more commonly known, involved it being formally passed round the High Table, but nothing

further is known. Such Grace Cups were originally used for the ceremonial masculine drinking of toasts or 'graces'. This cup, one of the oldest pieces of plate the college possesses, is a 1670 Charles II silver porringer (or small basin) inscribed with the college arms. Since the unity of the college had been damaged by the Civil War, the ceremony of passing the Loving Cup round the High Table daily had more than a symbolic significance. The custom was abolished in 1870 after the Cup had been in daily use for two hundred years. There is no trace of a Butler's Book in the college archives; the Buttery Books for the period survive but offer no clue. Perhaps the Butler kept a formal record of college guests or of all those who dined at High Table.

Mrs. Piozzi wrote to Duppa many years later:
"Of the dinner at University College I remember nothing, unless it was there that Mr. Vansittart, a flourishing sort of character, showed off his grateful form by fencing with Mr. Seward, who joined us at Oxford. We had a grand dinner at University College, and Dr. Johnson made Miss Thrale and me observe the ceremony of the grace cup; but I have but a faint remembrance of it, and can in nowise tell who invited us, or how we came by our academical honour of hearing our healths drank in form, and I half believe in Latin."

72. This was the Picture Gallery at Christ Church which has a fine collection of paintings and drawings, mostly 14th–17th c. Italian.

73. Mrs. Thrale visited the Clarendon Building (1713) which for many years was the university press. In 1830 it moved to larger premises in Walton Street.

74. New Inn Hall, in New Inn Hall Street, was founded about 1369 and closed in 1887. Sir Robert Chambers, a friend of Thrale's through Johnson, was a Fellow of University College and Vinerian Professor of Law from 1762 to 1777. In 1768 the Chancellor made him principal of New Inn Hall, a post which required no residence and which he held throughout his life. Thrale stayed with Chambers when Frederick, Lord North, the Prime Minister, was installed as Chancellor of Oxford University on 3 October 1772. Thrale again stayed with Chambers in July 1773, when he went up to receive his honorary degree of D.C.L.

75. This was Henry Thrale's property, Battle Farm, in Crowmarsh, so called because it was originally one of the lands given to Battle Abbey near Hastings as part of its endowment. After the Reformation the farm passed through various hands until it was eventually bought by Henry Thrale's father in 1742. It is still a flourishing farm today.

76. Charles Lowndes (1699-1783) of Chesham, Secretary to the Treasury.

77. William Burke was the cousin and companion of the great statesman and orator, Edmund Burke.

78. Ralph, Lord Verney was a Whig politician and Burke's patron; he was M.P. for Buckinghamshire, 1768-91.

Select Bibliography

A Diary of a Journey into North Wales in the Year 1774 by Samuel Johnson, LL.D., edited R. Duppa (1816). This is the first published edition of Johnson's Diary.
Dr. Johnson and Mrs. Thrale by A. M. Broadley. Bodley Head, 1909. This contains the only published version of Mrs. Thrale's Journal of her Tour in Wales with Dr. Johnson.
Boswell's Life of Johnson ed. George Birkbeck Hill, revised by L. F. Powell, in six volumes. Clarendon Press, Oxford, 1934-1964. Vol. V contains the most recent edition of Johnson's 'Welsh Diary'.
The Letters of Samuel Johnson, with Mrs. Thrale's genuine Letters to Him ed. R. W. Chapman. 3 Vols. Clarendon Press, Oxford 1952. Vol. I: 1719-1774.
Diaries, Prayers, and Annals ed. E. L. McAdam Jnr., with Donald and Mary Hyde. Yale University Press, 1958.
Hester Lynch Piozzi (Mrs. Thrale) by James L. Clifford. Oxford University Press, 1968.
The Thrales of Streatham Park by Mary Hyde. Harvard University Press, Cambridge, Mass., 1977.
Samuel Johnson by John Wain. Macmillan, 1980.
A Tour in Wales by Thomas Pennant (1778/81).
Wanderings in North Wales by Thomas Roscoe. C. Tilt and Simpkin & Co., Birmingham, 1836.
The Figure in the Landscape by John Dixon Hunt, The John Hopkins University Press, 1976.
English Gardens and Landscapes 1700-1750, by Christopher Hussey, Country Life Ltd., 1967.

Index

Illustrations are denoted by the use of italics.

Abergele	45.
Adams, Rev. Dr.	54, 81, 121.
Adderly Hall	64, 131.
Adey, Mary	57.
Arkwright, Richard	93, 96, 129-30.
Ashbourne	12, 22, 23, 26, 27, 32, 34, 60, 61, 91, 93, 94, 97, 130.
Astle, Captain	34, 62.
Aston, Miss Elizabeth	57, 90.
Bachygraig	11, 12, 18, 27, 37, 39, 66, 101, *102*, 103, 109, 119, 134.
Bachygraig Inheritance, The	11, 12, 18-9.
Bangor	23, 27, 45-6, 47, 50, 75, 111, 118.
Bangor Cathedral	50, 111, 118, 136.
Bardsey Island	77.
Baretti, Joseph	89, 127.
Barnet	31, 89.
Baron Hill	75, 111.
Battle Farm	141.
Beaconsfield	25, 86, 126.
Beaumaris	46-7, 51, 71, 75, 111.
Birmingham	12, 22, 23, 55, 123.
Blenheim Palace	56, 85, 140.
Bodfari	43, 44, 73, 107, 109, 134.
Bodfel Hall	12, 14, 15, 18, 47-8, 66, 114-5, *115*, 137, 138.
Bodryddan	105, 133.
Boswell, James	11, 14, 21, 22, 23, 24, 25, 27, 61, 140.
Boulton, Matthew	55, 85, 124, 140.
Bridge, Edward	18, 118, 119, 120, 134, 135.
Broadley, A.M.	21.
Brooke, Francis	128.
Brown, 'Capability'	33, 59, 61, 83, 85.
Bryant, Jacob	56, 85.
Brynbella	66, 132.
Brynodol	47, 48, 112, 113, 117, 137.
Bulkeley Family	46, 75, 111.
Bunbury, Henry	135.
Bunbury, Mrs. Catherine	109, 135.
Burke, Edmund	25, 56, 125-6.
Burleydam Chapel	98.
Buxton	34, 97, 130.
Caernarfon	47, 48, 49, 72, 77, 78, 112, 118.
Caernarfon Castle	47, *48*, 51, 71, 76, 112, 113.
Carless, Mrs.	140.
Cefnamwlch	49, 77, 116-7.
Chambers, Sir Robert	141.
Chatsworth	31, 59, 71, 92, 123.
Cheere, Sir Henry	70.
Chester	12, 27, 36, 42, 54, 65, 99, 100, 120.
Chester Castle	36, 103.
Chester Cathedral	36, 65, 100, 131.
Chirk Castle	52, 80, 120.
Clough, Sir Richard	66, 67, 68.
Clynnog Fawr	48, 77, 113, 117.
Cobb, Mrs. Thomas ('Moll')	31, 57, 91.
Collier, Mrs. Mary (née Dunn)	60.
Combermere Abbey	12, 15, 19, 34, 36, 63, 64, 65, 97, 99, 134.
Congleton	34.
Conwy	50-1, 71, 74, 78, 111.
Conwy Castle	78.
Conwy Races	74, 111.
Cotton, Frances	133.
Cotton, Hester Maria	105, 107, 110-11, 118.
Cotton, Hester (Hetty) Salusbury	131.
Cotton, Robert	12, 39, 64, 101, 104, 107, 120, 134.
Cotton, Sir Lynch Salusbury	12, 34, 36, 63, 64-5, 97, 98, 99.
Coulson, John	85, 125.
Croker, John Wilson	19-20.
Cromford	86, 125, 141.
Crowmarsh	125, 141.
Dale, Robert	60, 61.

Index   145

Dale, Mrs.	33, 94, 95.
Darwin, Erasmus	31, 57, 91.
D'Avenant, Corbet	99, 100, 108, 109, 110, 130-1, 134.
Davies, Mutton	69.
Davies, Robert	40, 69, 104.
Denbigh	11, 12, 38, 39, 66, 67-8, 72, 79, 80, 103-4, 105.
Dodwell, Henry	38, 67.
Dolbadarn Castle	49, *50*, 78.
Donegal, Lord	91, 128.
Dovedale	32, 33, 35, 94, 95, 129.
Dunstable	31, 89, 127.
Duppa, Richard	19, 25, 27, 65, 134.
Dyott, Catherine	60, 95.
Dyott, Richard	32, 33, 60, 94.
Dyserth	71, 105.
Eagle Tower, Caernarfon	47, 76, 112.
East Hyde	127.
Edensor	92.
Emes, William	75.
Essex, Earl of	68.
Evans, Evan (Ieuan Fardd)	42, 72.
Fisherwick	91, 128.
Flint, Mrs.	60.
Flint, Thomas	32, 60, 94.
Fort Williamsburg	*114*, 137.
Freeford Hall	60.
Friary, The	57, 91.
Garrick, David	58, 135.
Garrick, Peter	31, 58, 91, 128.
Gell, Philip	33, 60, 95-6.
Gilpin, Rev. William	61.
Gilpin, William	33, 61, 83, 94.
Glynllifon Park	113, 137.
Goldsmith, Oliver	110, 135-6.
Green, Richard	31, 57, 90, 91.
Greenfield Valley	71.
Gregories	25.
Griffith, Hugh	47, 49, 112, 113, 116, 117, 136.
Griffith, Madam Sidney	78.
Griffith, Mrs. Mary	112, 113, 136.
Griffith, John	77.
Guise, General John	124, 140.
Gwaynynog	23, 42, 50, 70, 72, 79, *105*, 105, *107*, 110, 118, 120.
Gwynn, John	81, 121.

Hagley Church	55, 83, 122.
Hagley Park	26, 55, 83, 122, 123.
Harris, Howel	78, 138.
Hawkstone Park	23, 35, 64, 99, 100.
Hector, Edmund	55, 56, 84, 123, 124, 140.
Hill, Miss	35, 36, 100.
Hill, Sir Rowland	35, 64, 98, 99.
Holywell	23, 40, 70, 71, 104-5.
Hopton Hall	60.
Hughes, David	75.
Ilam Hall	31, 35, 55, 92, 94, 110, 129.
Johnson, Samuel	passim.
his attitude to travel	11, 12.
his health	24.
history of his Diary	19.
its contents	22-5.
his views on the Tour	24.
his French Diary	22.
Kedleston	33, 61, 96, 123.
Kilmorey, Lord	34, 63, 98.
Kinver	54.
Lade, Lady	89, 127.
Langley, Rev. William	32, 33, 34, 61, 94.
Langton, Bennet	17, 95.
Leasowes, The	83-4, 123.
Leicester, The Earl of	38.
Levet, Robert	44, 74.
Lichfield	11, 12, 22, 23, 31, 43, 54, 57, 58, 60, 64, 73, 89-91, 127, 128.
Lichfield Cathedral	31, 90.
Little Hagley	81.
Llanfair Hall	48, 112, 136.
Llangwnnadl	47, 49, 138.
Llannerch	40, 69, 104.
Llannor	115, *116*, 138.
Llanrhaeadr-ym-Mochnant	52, 67, 80, 81, 139.
Lleweni Chapel	39, 68, 133.
Lleweni Hall	12, 15, 19, 23, 27, 35, 36-7, *37*, 43, 45, 64, 65, 73, 74, 99, *101*, 104, 110, 111, 118, 134.
Lleyn Peninsula	110, 135, 138.
Lloyd, Edward	42, 43, 46, 71, 73, 108, 120.
Lloyd, Rev. William	75.
Lloyd, Richard	115, 116, 138.
Lloyd, William, Bishop	38, 67.

146   Dr Johnson & Mrs. Thrale's Tour in North Wales 1774

Llwyd, Humphrey	39, 68.	Prys, Edmwnd	80.
Llyn Padarn	49.	Pwllheli	12, 18, 49, 66, 116, 138.
Llyn Peris	49, 117.		
Lowndes, Charles	126, 141.	Quarry, The	54, 81.
Lyttelton, Mrs. Caroline (née Bristow)	139.	Queeney (Thrale)	13, 18, 19, 22, 25, 78, 92,
Lyttelton, Sir Edward	55, 83, 95, 122.		93, 94, 99, 100, 105, 109, 110,
Lyttelton, Thomas, 2nd Lord	53, 55, 81, 82.		111, 113, 115, 117, 118, 123,
Lyttelton, W.H.	81, 83, 122.		124, 132, 135, 141.
		her character	15.
Macclesfield	34, 62, 97.	her character (by Mrs. Thrale)	26.
Maesmynnan	43, 73, 108, *108*, 120.		
Matlock	32, 92, 93, 94, 96, 129, 130.	Reynard's Cave	32, 60, 94.
Meynell, Hugo	94, 97, 130.	Reynolds, Joshua	109, 135.
Middlewich	34.	Rhuddlan Castle	41, 71, 105.
Mold	36, 70, 73, 101.	Rhys, Siôn Dafydd	42, 72.
Morgan, William, Bishop of St. Asaph	67, 80.	Roberts, Jack	50, 117.
Myddleton, Dr. Robert	19.	Roberts, Thomas	75.
Myddleton, John	42, 50, 51, 70, 72, 78-9,	Roscoe, Thomas	23.
	106, 118, *119*.	Rowlands, Henry	112-3. 136.
Myddelton, Rev. Robert	52, 79.	Ruthin	109.
Myddelton, Richard	80.	Rysbrack, Michael	131.
Nantwich	12, 34, 63.	St. Albans	89, 127.
Needham, John (Jack),10th Viscount Kilmorey		St. Asaph	27, 38, 51, 67, 68, 80, 103, 111.
	63, 98.	St. Beuno	70, 77.
Newton, Andrew	31, 57, 91.	St. Chad's Church	54, 81.
		St. Giles	53, 79.
Offley Place	15, 18, 19, 127, 134.	St. Hilary's Chapel	38, 68.
Okeover	31, 32, 59, 93, 95.	St. Mary's Church	76.
Okeover Chapel	32, 59, 93.	St. Oswald's Church	58, 80-1.
Okeover, Edward	59.	St. Winifride's Well	10, 10, 12, 70, 71, 101.
Ombersley	81.	Salusbury, John	14, 39, 138.
Oxford	11, 12, 22, 23, 56, 81, 86, 124,	Salusbury, Lady	89.
	125, 128, 131, 140-1.	Salusbury, Sir Thomas	12, 18-9, 89, 108,
			109, 119, 134.
Paoli, General Pasquale de	47, 76, 112, 113.	Sandys, Lady	121.
Parker, John	33, 61, 94.	Sandys, Lord	82, 121.
Parry, Mrs. Richard	109, 135.	Seward, Anna	31, 58.
Pengwern Hall	72.	Seward, William	124, 125, 140, 141.
Penmaenmawr	23, 27, 45, 50, 74-5, 111.	Shavington Hall	63, 98.
Penmaen-Rhos	45, 51.	Shenstone, William	55, 83-4, 123.
Pennant, Thomas	65-6, 72, 137.	Shipley, Dr. Jonathan, Bishop of St. Asaph	
Piozzi, Gabriel	127.		67, 133, 134.
Piozzi, Mrs. Hester (see Thrale, Mrs. Hester)		Shipley, Mrs. Ann (née Mordaunt)	132, 134.
Pistyll Rhaeadr	121.	Shipley, Mrs. Penelope (née Yonge)	133.
Plasnewydd	112, 136.	Shipley, William, Dean of St. Asaph	134.
Plygain		Shrewsbury	12, 23, 27, 52, 81, 120, 121, 124.
Pontruffyd		Silk Mill, Derby	33.
Poole's Cavern	34, 62, 100.	Silk Museum, Macclesfield	62.
Porter, Miss Lucy	57, 90, 91.	Smith, Ralph	89, 127.

Index 147

Snowdon	27, 49, 78, 112, 117, 120.
Southwark	25, 126.
Stapleton	42.
Streatham	15, 17, 18, 22, 25, 31, 76, 89, 126.
Swan Hotel	31, 57.
Taylor, Dr. John (Shrewsbury)	11, 58, 81.
Taylor, Rev. Dr. John (Ashbourne)	12, 27, 31, 91, 92, 93, 94, 97.
Thomson, James	83.
Thoyt's Copper Mill	105, 133.
Thrale, Henry	11-2, *14*, 15.
his character	13.
his character (by Mrs. Thrale)	13, 14, 22.
his character (by Johnson)	13.
his death	127.
Thrale, Hester Maria, later Lady Keith (see Queeney)	
Thrale, Mrs. Hester (née Salusbury)	11-2, *16*, 18, 19, 23, 24.
her feelings about the Tour	26-7.
her character	14-5.
history of her Journal	21, 25.
its nature	21-2.
her disappointment with the Tour	26.
becomes Mrs. Piozzi	127.
Thrale, Ralph	15, 82, 109, 128.
Tremeirchion	39, 104, 132.
Troughton, Lt. Ellis, R.N.	47, 76, 117.
Tudweiliog	49, 138.
Tynewydd	115, 116, 138.

Vansittart, Dr. Robert	56, 85, 125.
Verney, Lord	126, 142.
Yyse, Miss Mary	31, 58.
Vyse, Rev. W.	58.
Walhouse, Edward	59.
Walpole, Horace	72, 135.
Wenlock	54.
West Malling (Town Malling)	128
Whistler, Rex	136.
Whitchurch (Eglwys Wen)	66, 68, 104.
White, Rev. Henry	19.
Wood, Mrs. Mary	34, 62.
Woodstock	56, 124.
Worcester Cathedral	54, 121.
Worthington, Rev. William	42, 47, 52, 72, 80.
Wrenbury	63.
Wrexham	27, 52, *53*, 80, 120.
Wynn, Lady Catherine	113.
Wynn, Mrs. Bridget	49, 77, 113, 117, 118.
Wynn, Sir Thomas (later Lord Newborough)	47, 76, 112, 113, 136.
Wynne, Dr. William	131.
Yale, Elihu	80.
Yorke, Mr.	72.
Yonge, Mr.	107.

Bridge Books are specialist publishers of history books with a particular emphasis upon Welsh History, Local History, Military History and Aviation History. If you would like a catalogue listing all of our current publications please write to:—

Bridge Books, Wingett House, 25a Chester Street, Wrexham, LL13 8BG.